Rachel Birkbeck had degrees from both Sunderland and Leeds Metropolitan Universities in historical studies and higher education, respectively. She taught at Newcastle College and The Manchester College, and at HMP Acklington and HMP Castington (now HMP Northumberland) before pursuing her dream career in dog handling. Rachel worked as a dog psychologist and lived at home with her wife, two dogs, four cats, and a goldfish before sadly passing away in October 2021.

For all cancer warriors and their armies.

Rachel Birkbeck

MONGRELS VERSUS PEDIGREES

Fighting Cancer the 'She-Wolf' Way

AUSTIN MACAULEY PUBLISHERS™

LONDON · CAMBRIDGE · NEW YORK · SHARJAH

A CIP catalogue record for this title is available from the British Library.

ISBN 9781528981729 (Paperback)
ISBN 9781528981736 (ePub e-book)

www.austinmacauley.com

First Published 2023
Austin Macauley Publishers Ltd®
1 Canada Square
Canary Wharf
London
E14 5AA

I would like to extend my thanks and gratitude to my specialists in Oncology and Chemotherapy at the Queen Elizabeth Hospital. You have all made 'me' possible and made this book possible to support other sufferers.

Chapter One

They say laughter is the best medicine. To be honest, I agree! Life isn't always a barrel of laughs granted; things are thrown at us that makes us wonder, ponder, challenge us, torment us, and make us cry, and worry or panic. These things are a natural part of life. How we cope with these challenges is what makes the difference to our outlook on life in general. Are we half or full glass people? Optimists or pessimists? Negative or positive?

I have myself been through some difficult challenges that have in fact broken me into pieces (I'm human that way, just like everyone else), but I have had love and laughter through it all and gotten through the other side. I wanted to share some of those experiences with you and help you all see the humorous side of life, because there is in fact humour in everything, especially if you have a filthy mind like mine!

It is important to remember that we are all born out of darkness, the dark of the womb and it's up to us to seek the light. Much like if we are currently in a place of negativity, it is merely a starting point to the positive. We all begin from negativity when a challenge besets us, but it doesn't have to define our journey through that challenge.

As we begin this journey let us ponder upon the aptness of this beautiful prayer: *God grant me the serenity to accept the things I cannot change, to change the things that I can, and the wisdom to know the difference.* Amen.

I began this particular journey twenty-five years ago, from a place of negativity, fear and grief. I was fourteen years old and my twenty-six-year-old, beautiful aunt Barbara had been diagnosed with Non-Hodgkin's Lymphoma. I visited her in the hospital every night that I could where she shared a ward with another young woman, with whom she became friends. The young woman sharing the room passed away after years of fighting. It was very difficult for my aunt, and she became increasingly fearful. She was young and afraid, failing in her health, unable to do the job she loved, as a chef. She had lost her beautiful hair and it embarrassed her. She was painfully thin and the chemotherapy made her sick. She received radiotherapy too. On her twenty-sixth birthday, she had been in remission and having the sense of humour that she did joke to her family that the cancer had come back. We were furious when she burst out laughing saying she was just joking. Unfortunately, a few days later after another scan, she had unwittingly been correct. The cancer had in fact come back. My father gently informed my brother and me of her passing, I was hysterical. I ran to comfort my mother. I must have looked ridiculous when I recall how I ran into the kitchen where the family friends were: I had ears stuffed with cotton wool and olive oil with a Santa hat pulled down over my ears to keep the fluff in, fluffy pyjamas with a heavy bathrobe on top, a Rudolph Red nose, a voice like Rod Stewart and hysterical tears streaming down my face. Not that I gave a flying f*** how I looked and neither did they!

My aunts' passing utterly devastated me. I just didn't understand. My brain couldn't cope with it. I couldn't sleep that night. My mother found me at six o'clock in the morning lying in the foetal position in front of the fire in the living room sobbing. Nothing could make me understand why she had been taken. I couldn't find peace in my brain. I feared death. I feared cancer. I feared illness. Nothing seemed worth it anymore if a twenty-six–year-old lady who didn't smoke, rarely drank, ate healthy, exercised regularly and had a good job that she loved, could be so cruelly taken from us. Although I didn't comprehend, I never blamed anyone or anything. Everything had been done to save her that could be done.

Obviously, I went back to school after the Christmas Holidays. I attended Catholic schools, being a Roman Catholic. My friends inevitably asked if I had a good Christmas and the obvious answer was 'no'. When I told one of my friends what had happened, she asked if the service had been nice. I told her I had been too hysterical and poorly to attend. I had attended the service the previous evening to perform the Roman Catholic ritual of receiving her body into the Church. Seeing the cars and her coffin and feeling the way I did, I chose not to attend her funeral the next day. My friend asked how I coped. I replied that I had gone to church the day before and lit candles and prayed for her. She said defiantly, 'When my uncle died, my aunt stopped going to church. God could have saved him.' She then went on to explain how her uncle had refused all treatments offered to him. I didn't follow her aunt's logic! Had she never heard the saying *'God helps those who helps themselves'*. We have to meet God halfway; if he offers us a lifeboat, we have to get in it! It never occurred to me to blame God for taking my aunt! S*** happens. My aunt was now safe and at peace amongst the angels, with God. What better honour for the innocent lambs of this world!

I've never gotten over her loss, as has none of the family. It was my first experience of losing a loved one to whom I was so close. I now view her passing with a whole new understanding and philosophy after years of self-analysis. I cannot change it, so I accept it with a whole new understanding: my own understanding which works well for me in my belief system.

It turns out that her passing was her biggest parting gift to me; it just took me years to understand the gift (well, that's just me, she knew I'd get it eventually!) Her death left me in a place of great personal devastation and negativity. I was totally in the dark with life; lost, and hopeless and pointless. It was a terrifying place to be. It took me a long time, but this was to be the beginning of my journey into the light and towards positivity.

Allow me to explain! I always felt a bit awkward and out of place as a child. I didn't like the things that other girls liked: the clothes, the makeup, the jewellery, the dolls etc. I liked trousers and boots, cats and animals, reading, going to church, playing football and hanging out with the lads. I was the only girl, amongst a brother and two male cousins. I gravitated to them and not the girls at school who just picked on me. The only female friend I had at primary school was another girl who played football with her older brothers, but she was still into all the pretty feminine things and hung out with the other trendy girls, when they were around rather than me. I remember being alone a lot in the playground when I was about four or five years old. This did not stop me however from enjoying my education. I had an excellent relationship with my teachers and I loved learning as a naturally inquisitive child. I was the first in my class to fully master reading and writing and once I got a taste for books, I had to be dragged kicking and screaming from the library! If I was offered friendship, I took it, but didn't actually seek it for fear of rejection. I was a shy, sensitive and timid child. I would not sing or dance in public as I felt I was less able than the other children and didn't want to be made more fun of.

I remember during a school assembly, my headmistress talking to us about making strangers feel welcome i.e., new pupils. A new pupil was joining us during the week and we were basically asked to befriend him. When he arrived, he was loitering around the playground on his own. On this rare occasion, I was talking to my female friend who was hanging out with the trendy girls (there were only five girls in my class of thirty-three pupils). I could see he was on his own so I approached him and offered him friendship as we had been instructed. As we were talking to each other and I invited him into our group, my footballing female friend and her trendy mates grabbed hold of me and threw me into the nearest bush, holding me there and laughing at me saying 'What are you doing talking to him?' I said, he was on his own and needed company. They pushed me further into the bush and left me there to get out on my own. The poor new lad had fled, frightened, and gone and sat by himself. I saw his face as I struggled out of the bush. He looked helpless and hopeless, afraid to assist me. He looked as equally lost as I felt. We rarely spoke again, but we seemed to have a silent, unspoken connection and we silently protected each other when we could.

A little while later, he was suddenly absent from school. In assembly, we were told that he was due back soon and to be supportive of him as he had just lost his mother in tragic and unforeseen circumstances (we later learnt that she had dropped dead in the street from a brain haemorrhage whilst doing the family shop). We were all eight years old. I went home very upset that evening and confided to my parents why I was upset. They were incredibly supportive, as my parents are!

The young man eventually came back to school and we greeted him with a hug and welcomed him back with support. Then during a particular exercise in class where we had been split into groups to work out a puzzle, an altercation broke out between the grieving boy and another pupil. The grieving boy reacted angrily and the other boy stood up, threw his papers at him and screamed in front of the whole class, 'I'm glad your mother died!' The young man ran out in tears. It was a cruel and heartless statement. The whole class fell silent in horror. My teacher left me and my friend to look after the class while she took the young boy to another teacher who was not teaching. When she came back a few moments later, we were all still frozen solid and she took the insulting pupil to one side and brought him to his knees in tears with shame. He was fully prepared to apologise and repent the matter to the young boy. The young grieving lad came back in and the teacher took them off privately for a discussion. Both had been going through a hard time at home and things had just come to a head and angry hurtful words were thrown. The boy who had insulted the griever was horrified at his own words. They remained friends.

However, I went home very upset that night. I couldn't believe a child would be glad when another's loved one had died! I couldn't imagine being without my parents! All kinds of thoughts went through my sensitive little brain (I have a titchy head, even as an adult! No seriously, it's only twenty-two inches in circumference-child size!) My parents, as usual, were lovely and explained that sometimes when people are angry or upset, they say horrible things they don't mean but usually apologise when they realise how horrible they were. At this point, I told them about my friends pushing me in the bush when I had tried to befriend him. I was asked if they were just playing and messing about. I said I didn't think so because they didn't help me out and neither did they apologise. I was advised that real friends don't do that kind of thing; yes, there's rough and tumble but if anyone gets hurt inadvertently the offender is supposed to apologise and make amends. I kept my distance from such people from then and became even more of a loner from my classmates. I didn't trust them to be nice.

I found a friend in a younger pupil who had joined our school. She was a year younger than I but became a member of my year group because she just fit into the age bracket for my class, so she was the youngest and most vulnerable. She was sporty and intelligent and for some reason gravitated towards me; maybe because she saw a kindred spirit and I welcomed friendship although did not seek it. She was an honest and lovely girl and I felt very protective of her. We had a great deal of fun together playing Rounders and Catch. I dare say, she made me feel purposeful. She would hug me a lot; this was a new experience for me; my 'friends' didn't hug me, but she clung onto me for life itself it seemed. I think I was nine years old.

Then one day at school we were playing on the grass and I was watching the girls and my new friend practicing cartwheels together (I sat it out being too shy and totally crap at them!) One of the girls inadvertently kicked my friend beneath the chin with her heel as they cartwheeled together and my friend ended up biting her own tongue. There was blood everywhere. The girl who had accidently kicked her ran over to see what had happened and my friend said, (with a mouthful of blood) 'You caught me under the chin'. Blood was spewing out of her mouth. One of the other girls ran for a teacher. But another girl, the class bully grabbed hold of my friend screaming (for a nine-year-old!) 'You fucking cunt!!! Don't blame her,' and proceeded to beat her! My friends and I ran to help her but when the bully saw the teacher approaching, she backed off and found me comforting my crying bleeding friend as best I could. She hadn't blamed or provoked anyone! It had been an accident!

The girl who had accidently kicked her and the bully had been taken off for scrutiny over the matter, my friend got rushed to hospital for a severe laceration to her tongue, and two other girls and myself were taken to the headmistress to discuss the incident. We all agreed that the kick had been completely accidental and that the girl who kicked her hadn't seen where my friend was or realised what had happened. But when it came to reporting the actions of the bully, I was the only one to tell the truth. The other girls were afraid of her and didn't want to make too much of it. I was having otherwise!!! My friend had been deliberately beaten after the accident by the school bully, and I was not prepared to stand by and let her get away with it! The other girl's sugar coated it, saying it was purely verbal, but some of the lads playing football had seen the bully attack the girl and backed me up.

A little while later, I remember sitting at the sink in my classroom washing paint brushes and palettes after my artwork and the classroom door suddenly burst open. The bully's mother (being escorted out of the building by a teacher after a meeting about her bullying daughter) had seen me at the sink and filled with fury decided to burst in and scream at me across the room. 'It's your fault Rachel bloody BIRKBECK that my daughter isn't allowed on the school trip. I'll have you and your f***ing mother too!' The teacher escorting her dragged her away kicking and screaming while my own teacher ran to me in horror asking if I was ok. I was frozen with terror! I had never been threatened by an adult before!!! And to threaten my own mother!!! I wasn't worried about me. I knew my parents and teachers would protect me. But who would protect my parents? My mother! I was only a little powerless girl! I obviously confided in my parents what had transpired and how afraid for them I was. As always they reassured me and nothing more was mentioned of such incident. I unfortunately never saw my friend again as her mother transferred her to a different school because of the bully.

You may now be wondering what the f*** I'm waffling on about, but I assure you there is a point. The point is I had a beautiful and wonderful home life filled with love and positivity from everyone I met within that circle. At school, this is where I met with negativity and was made to feel different by others. The negativity was not mine; it was thrust upon me by others. When I showed compassion, I was considered abnormal, soft and a target for bullies. It seriously knocked my confidence about meeting new people and making friends on my own, but it didn't change who I am as a person inside and the principles, and qualities I hold dear because I always returned to love from a negative situation or experience. I always returned to my family. A family filled with love, compassion, generosity, faith, humility, wisdom, advice, support, affection, loyalty and devotion. There was always light at the end of any darkness I experienced and every day was a new gift, and a new challenge to make a difference to someone.

I kind of found a place at a senior school where things made sense after a rough start. I wasn't used to making friends actively, so I found it a challenge at first and I although I remained unique and quite individual in myself, I fell in with friends who might have, at the time, not quite seemed to have fit into the 'norm' themselves: I made friends with the girl in class who had superior brain power, and an unusual personality; I made friends with the self-image obsessed girl; I made friends with the fun-loving girl who was a bit shy and self-conscious; I made friends with the girl who was less academically able who was quite worldly-wise in other matters. My point is, although we were all very different in very different ways, we had a bond that united us. We didn't go around causing trouble. We worked hard, looked after each other, pursued interests together or separately without judgement. I had many male friends too (I had always gotten on well with men folk, having grown up in a male oriented family and playing football with my male friends on a daily basis). Women were a bit of mystery to me! I just didn't understand them! I think that's why I was a bit of an odd ball at school!

There was a clique (as there inevitably always is!) of girls who defy and push the boundaries and think they can just do what they want without consequences. These are the girls who had to have the latest gear, wear make up to school, wear jewellery to school, wear trainers to school, wear high heels if they want, roll their skirts up to their arses and leave their ties undone and top buttons open to the breast! (None of which the school allowed for obvious reasons!) These girls were despicable violent bullies who preyed on the most vulnerable students. Every student was a target though and at some point on the end of their poisonous words. I was no exception to that, and neither were my friends. They were constantly in bother with teachers etc. and they just did not care. The best course of action for us was to just ignore them and walk away. Why give a bully an argument to use as ammunition against you? I wasn't in the habit of inviting a fight so why bother? So yeah, I was bullied at senior school in some form too, just like everyone else was.

And here comes my repentance, publicly and without reservation. There was a young man in some of my classes who was incredibly talented and gifted, sensitive, funny and kind. I liked him a lot. At the time, he was small for his age, and he was bullied excessively. On more than one occasion I participated in taunting him, despite my love and respect for him. I could proffer 'reasons' but they are merely excuses that are inexcusable and I greatly sinned against this young man. I bumped into him a few years after we had all left school, and I was delighted to see him. I thought he might be horrified to see me however. I was wrong! We met and hugged with gusto. After, the usual greetings I offered to buy him a drink. I wanted to talk to him. I apologised profusely for any participation at school that caused pain and suffering for him. He shrugged and said, 'Just kids being kids.' I was mortified! I felt awful! I said that I knew on occasions, I had not been very nice to him, and that I was well out of order, and I was deeply sorry. He seemed to have dealt with it all so well! He said he barely remembered me being nasty to him. All he really remembered was our friendship when we were away from the bullies. Even though, I reminded him that my actions were sinful and inexcusable and, that I regretted my despicable behaviour towards him very deeply. He said he knew. He seemed to have an enlightened understanding and forgave me on the spot, although, I did not deserve his mercy.

He and I are friends to this day. He is a very talented, funny, intelligent, gifted, loving and compassionate man. I am humble before his mercy and forgiveness. He reminds me of the very talented actor, Steve Buscemi. I wish my friend to know that my repentance is true and honest from a genuine heart who repents fully of her sin against you.

I was bullied and taunted at school but that is no excuse for repeating the behaviour on someone else just because you feel powerless and need a target to control and take your frustration out on. I changed somewhat when my beloved aunt passed over, and it reflected in my anger and frustration when I went back to school and I displayed a nasty side to the 'weakest'. Like all bullies, I must have sub-consciously sought control of something and someone to blame. I did not realise it at the time. My mind blamed no one but my emotions obviously needed an outlet and this manifested negatively. My aunts' passing affected me deeply. I had never felt so angry, fearful, lost and hopeless. I had no one to talk to about it. My friends didn't really care or understand how close we were. My mother was already going through hell and for the first time in my life, I felt unable to confide in her. My brother and I hadn't even been able to attend the funeral as we were both very upset and me on the verge of hysteria. I felt overlooked and ignored, like how I felt wasn't important. I felt like it was a matter of 'just get on with it Rach' we're all grieving the same way. I was massively protected from the truth (not that I hold anyone accountable for that as they did what they thought was right at the time), so my aunt's passing over came as a horrific shock to me.

From that moment I was swallowed by a negativity that was my own; not a negativity that had come from outside. This was a new battle. I knew how to defend myself from outside negativity, I had been doing it for years and succeeding. But now, I was trapped inside my head space and failing miserably. I must admit that it's a battle I still fight, but this time I always win! I felt very alone, abandoned, grieving, lost and unsupported. I now know this probably wasn't the case, but I was afraid, and destroyed inside and not thinking straight (not that I ever have!) I remained silently wounded for a long time. But things started to change.

I said earlier, that my aunt had given me a last parting gift. It was to be the beginning of my recovery. There is a point to all this: I promise! Sorry if I bored the crap out of you in the meantime!

I met a wonderful friend called Clare, younger than I, in my brother's year at school. I believe we met on the school bus? I seriously cannot remember because I have just loved her ever since and regarded her as the sister I never had. She's not just a friend, she's family. We just clicked! We are both very different people, but I had a sudden need to protect her, like an older sister. She made me realise that over the years I had seen many of my friends suffer at the hands of tormentors and with the death of my aunt, I had inadvertently become one myself. I had to repent and protect her. It was just instinctual; a love and bond I could not explain but I knew that I would lay my life down for this girl to protect her.

My dear friend was bullied at school and one day she sought me out in the common room where I was a Sixth Form student; lower school weren't allowed in, so she asked for me. I went to her, and she told me that she had been threatened with physical violence and by whom. I wanted her to be left alone; she had done nothing wrong. I held her hand tightly and asked her to lead me to where the bullies were. We found them. I asked my friend to stay out of sight and I began a discussion with the bullies. I was not afraid (for a change!) I said angrily 'Right, who threatened her and why?' A tall girl came forward, all full of herself 'I just told her not to sit it my seat on the bus home, or I'd bray her'. I asked her which seat, and she responded with 'The front one next to the driver.' I laughed in her face! Unofficially that seat belonged to the school prefects (of which I was one) and so was one of my other sixth form friends. I was very protective of my dear friend Clare, and she shared our seat; if there was no space on the seat, I would hold her on my lap like a big sister. And this upstart had physically manhandled my friend and threatened her with violence! I responded to this lanky bully 'You won't be sitting in that seat on the way home. I'll be there before you anyway. You've never sat it in before and you won't be sitting in it now,' She responded with 'If I find you in my seat,

I'll kick you all over'. I laughed and walked away saying 'Will you now?'

I was on the bus in my seat with my prefect friend as per usual and my little sister friend, Clare got on. There was no room left on the seat so, she took up her usual protective position upon my knee. She was scared about the bully. I put my arms around her and reassured her. I wasn't the bully's target, my friend was and I would do anything to protect her. The bully eventually boarded the bus and saw us in the seat. Immediately she shouted, 'What are you doing in my seat?' I calmly responded that this wasn't her seat. But she demanded to sit there. I refused to move. She criticised the fact that my friend was sitting on my lap 'She's in my seat! She needs to move and so do you. I'll kick your heads' in!' I didn't budge and held my friend tighter. I said 'Ok, go and kick my head in. In front of everyone on the bus. However, I wouldn't want you to be embarrassed by someone who has martial arts training'. The bully stopped threatening me but challenged my friend to a fight that night after school, saying she'd be watching and waiting for her. I said I'd see her there. I would protect my friend at all costs!

Anyways, I went to my friends' street at the appointed hour preparing to defend her against this bully who seemed intent on harming her. I informed my friend I was there and waiting. And so I waited and waited...for an hour and a half. The bully was a no show. My friend and I spent the rest of the evening listening to music and eating noodles! I reassured her and went home.

The next day, we were on the bus. I was in my usual seat and my friend was in in her usual place on my lap. The bully got on. My friend tensed. The bully said, 'Morning'. She looked awful. I asked if she was alright and said I'd waited for her. She just shook her head and said she didn't feel well. Again I asked her what was wrong and she thought she had a tummy bug. She really did look awful. I took her hand and invited her to sit next to me on 'the seat'. My friend stood up to make way, also concerned. I comforted the bully as best I could until we got to school and advised her to speak to her form tutor immediately. As far as I know the bully got sent home poorly that day and was not on the school bus that night.

When she came back, however it was a different story. She had gotten on the school bus before us prefects and when we arrived, she was in 'our' seat. She immediately arose and said, 'I kept your seat for you!' She was jubilant. We gave our thanks and invited her to join us. On getting to know her she was just a girl seeking acceptance anyway she could, whether it was through fighting, arguing, bullying or defiance; she just wanted to be noticed. She was a really nice girl deep inside but who had been surrounded by negativity and abuse. She ended up sitting on my other knee on 'the seat' next to my darling friend on occasions.

Deep down I suppose I knew that the bully was wounded and didn't really want to fight us. She was fighting herself. That did not stop me from being prepared to fight for my own family and friends. I found a new self-confidence.

The trust that Clare had put in me gave me a sense of purpose. To protect and serve. I know that I sound like some cop slogan when I say that but the service came first and with service comes protection. Clare changed my life and my outlook. I began to understand a bit more about myself. Yes, I still had my own personal battles go on in my tiny little napper, but I seemed to have more control over things and more positivity in my life.

A few of my friends were suffering in their own way at the time and I was heartbroken by one particular situation. I broke down on my dad's lap after he noticed how gloomy and defeated I was. I was utterly ripped apart for my unhappy friend. We later found happiness together in a martial arts class (I did not fib earlier about my martial arts skills! It's a Commandment: Thou shalt not bear false witness). Although I did not know how to help my friend, my father said, 'Do what you can darling, that's all you can do. I know you love her and will be there for her if she needs you. And we will be here for you too'. It was a difficult time for me because I had become so jealously protective of my friends and family. The positivity went a bit far and I became stupidly possessive. Possessiveness is not healthy and I recognised this rapidly. I didn't want negativity. I needed positivity emanating from me, not horrid things!

Life became suddenly different for me at the age of seventeen years old, in a spiritual kind of way. I had always been heavily involved with the church; I read at Mass from the age of eight years old. The service mesmerised me. I just got it all. I seemed to just understand and want to know more. The parish priest was a regular feature at my school and, I was under his spell at Mass. He came around to choose his male altar servers. I was wounded! I wanted to serve. I dreamt of becoming a priest. But it was not possible. In that day, girls were not even allowed on the boys' football pitch at school, let alone serve at the Holy Eucharistic Feast!

I used to watch the Snooker with my father, who was an excellent player. I worshiped my father and still do. When I was little, I would say 'Wasn't that a good snook Daddy?' in excitement. My dad would smile and hug me tighter saying 'Yes, darling' even if it were a crap snook! One night he was discussing with my younger brother how he would introduce him to the committee of the club when he came of age and how he would be a full member just like his dad before him etc. My brother wasn't too fussed, but I was mightily offended! I asked my father why I couldn't be affiliated when I came of age? He said, it was because I was female. I was outraged! I wasn't even a teenager at this point! My father felt outraged too. He did not agree with the out-dated rules but told me that was how it was for the time being and that it didn't mean anything really. He still taught me how to play darts, snooker and pool etc. My father was not a religious man; spiritual and honourable yes; he agreed with me that women should be allowed to serve on the altar and treated as equals. Inequality horrified him. I always have a point by the way! So bear with the brain!

Anyway, it was one Easter when I was about nine years old. I was very serious about my faith and devotion. I had failed to be chosen as an altar server based solely upon my gender. I was wounded. Back in the day, they showed devotional films over religious feasts, not the frivolous crap you get nowadays. So there's me. All my mates are out playing football etc. and where am I? I am lying on the floor in the living room with my duvet and munchies watching The Robe. My parents had been busy in the kitchen prepping dinner, watching the kids outside as much as they could, assuming I was in my room reading if I wasn't in the mood for activity. My dad only realised where I was when he came to check his race results on teletext (as it was back in the day!)

I heard him tip toe out, my eyes and ears still glued to the movie. He came back with my mother moments later and whispered, 'She hasn't moved! What is she watching?' My mam, recognising the movie replied, 'She's watching The Robe, leave her be. She's transfixed.' My dad responded with, 'I've never seen such a devoted and faithful child. She really believes, doesn't she?' I will never forget those words of my father, whispered behind me as they tried not to disturb my own little form of worship. My mother replied in a whisper, 'Yes, she does.' And they were right as per usual!

There is a point to this background, I promise! I'm not just waffling like a brainless twat! At the age of seventeen I was given an opportunity to participate more fully in my faith in the form of the Young Christian Workers. A representative came and spoke at my school, and I was hooked. I had found a niche. Not to bore you or anything, but I attended weekly prayer meetings with my group of YCW friends and go for a pint afterwards with our chaplain. It might sound tedious to some who have not experienced that kind of fellowship, but the YCW were some of the most formative people during my teenage years. We had awesome times and on one of our retreats I learned a very valuable lesson. It was a lesson on self-worth and being able to appreciate a compliment and its value to the soul. Most of us did not know how to take a compliment as we did not recognise our self-worth. We learned a great deal about each other and ourselves after the exercise, where we were challenged to compliment everyone for something we appreciated about them, and they had to learn to accept it and say thank you and give something positive about them back.

I discovered about myself that I am apparently funny, charming, generous, helpful, compassionate, loyal, knowledgeable, playful, and inoffensive, protective, devoted to my faith and that my love of Queen was mutually shared by all! I gave thanks to all and praised God.

It was an epiphany for me. I no longer felt worthless and helpless. I had a place with the Lord. I was filled with light. Suddenly, the fearful and shy child who would not sing or dance was planning a Queen act with a friend to perform in front of our group! I was to be Freddie Mercury and my new friend was to be Brian May. As he was making his curly wig (from a dust mask and black ribbons!) we chatted on. He had survived Non-Hodgkin's Lymphoma. He was only nineteen years old and said he was unable to have children because of the chemotherapy. I was gutted for him but pleased he had overcome it. I told him about my aunt passing from the same. He was devastated for me. We talked about it and I randomly asked him, 'Did you ever blame God?' He said, 'Good Lord no! You just stay strong and believe in Him! I'm here now being Brian May!'

That night we went out and rocked it! We started the show in darkness, with the drums of We Will Rock You, dressed as 'Brian' and 'Freddie' and strutted down the aisle. Lighters were in the air in the darkness as the drums rolled on and the music started. Suddenly, I started singing *We Will Rock You* dressed as Freddie Mercury in front of a crowd of people I had only met in the last week! Unheard of!!! We did three songs and got a standing ovation! It was life changing!

Me and my friend however could not remove our makeup! My 'tash had been painted on in layers with thick acrylic black paint. Getting it off was a disaster and messy! My teeth were black for days! And neither could we remove the grey eye shadow on our faces which we had used for stubble effect. It didn't look too bad on my male friend...that is until he shaved! I laughed frantically when I saw him...until I looked in the mirror and saw with horror that I looked like Julian Clary after a heavy night on the drink!

I went back home looking like a rather distinguished male version of myself! It was freaking hilarious! Luckily, my parents and brother were on holiday so, didn't see me looking like a fella for the next week! And it was the holidays and I was waiting to start university, so I went into hiding!

It was a life changing experience that week away. I made new friends in ways I never thought possible. I found my inner confidence and my faith became more defined. This was followed up with a visit to Paris for the World Youth Day 1997 under Pope John Paul II. It was truly awe inspiring. My friend and I stayed with a very affluent, French couple who treated us like royalty. They had a lovely little Yorkshire Terrier called Rupert. They gave us free reign to come and go to events, Mass, prayer meetings, tours and visits etc. and took us on a tour themselves.

I made new friends worldwide, exchanged prayer cards and blessings, shared devotions and prayers with them. The feeling of unification and love was intense. It was pure peace. I can't tell you how many times, I cried with pure love. It was extremely intense.

I made a new friend in a retired headmaster, with whom I visited the Eiffel Tower. He wanted to ascend and wanted company, so I went with him, even though I am in mortal fear of heights! We stood and queued for two hours in blazing heat. The closer I got and looked up, my vertigo kicked in.

The view from beneath the tower was beautiful and incredible, but I started to sway, and my resolve weakened. Peter held my hand and told me to be brave. I was a nervous wreck!!! I was sweating and shaking with fear. Finally, we approached the steps up…

I ascended the first two steps with shaking legs and bated breath. Peter said, 'You'll be fine, just don't look down'. Well, I'm the type of moron who does exactly just that…I bloody well only went and looked down didn't I? To my horror, the stairs were filled with holes, being those old cast iron types. I could see the ground and knew that if I ascended further, I would see the growing height and space appearing before us. I'm not very good with heights (or bridges for that matter, yeah, I'm weird like that!) Well, I freaked out and ran away! I was petrified! Peter found me and I apologised profusely for ruining his experience. He wasn't bothered. He was starting to waver himself it appears! He could have laughed at me and made fun of my fear; I had suffered that before, but he was deeply compassionate and didn't make me feel ashamed or embarrassed. He empathised with me. It was quite a new experience for me from someone who had been a total stranger only a few days before.

Paris was where I experienced the true humanity of the world. The love and unity that was meant to be for all. I was truly uplifted. I came home absolutely buzzing. I was bouncing with joy when I started university. I made friends easily at university with my new-found confidence and trust.

That was to come crashing the down around me a year later. I won't go into details about it as it is no longer relevant, but I will discuss as to the state in which it left me because that part is. I lost my confidence, my self-identity, my ability to trust and my ability to distinguish between someone who can be helped and someone who cannot; someone who is a true soul and someone who is a false soul. I became suspicious, self-loathing and lost my ability to follow my own instincts. Having lost my confidence, I lost my ability to trust my own self. It was a dark place to be.

I found solace in the arms of a woman with three beautiful children. I fell in love with them all. I spent a lot of time with the children doing fun and happy things and being a mother to them. When they hurt, I hurt. I was a parent…but also a glorified babysitter. My partner was a violent, cheating and abusive drunk with her own damaging issues. I supposed I stayed as long as I did because I loved the children and being with them and genuinely believed that if I loved her enough, she would change. She became so violent towards me that I ended up being afraid to be around her, so I avoided her; each time I had tried to leave her she would find any means to draw me back, so I basically began in working ridiculous amounts of overtime just to stay away from her. She eventually left me for someone else. I suppose I was a coward doing it that way, but I didn't know what else to do.

Transitioning away from my children and my dog was difficult indeed. I missed them on a daily basis. I had lost my routine of getting them up and dressed on a morning, making sure their uniforms were ready for school and that they had packed lunches and a hot meal for when they came home. I would help them with homework, bathe them, wash their hair and do puppet shows with Boris the tiger at bed time. I'd comfort them if they had a nightmare or an upset. I'd do anything at all for them. And now all that was gone. I admit I was completely lost!

There was no one there for me however, when the nightmares about my ex terrified me. She was always a zombie in my nightmares trying to attack me. I know it sounds crazy, but I am terrified of zombies and have been since childhood when I had a horrible nightmare about zombies. Where it came from, I have no idea, but I've been monstrously afraid ever since! I became terrified to shut my eyes!

As you might imagine I was in a very vulnerable state still, when a few months later, I met my next partner. She was younger than I and just out of university, but she was taller and broader than I. I already knew her as a friend of a friend. Turned out she had liked me for a while! She was incredibly protective over me and she made me feel valuable. We had fun together. One night on the way home from a night out she told me that she had always found me attractive and confident but thought I was 'well out of her league'. I laughed and said, 'Really?' She said, 'When I first met you when I was with my ex and when she introduced you as her ex-girlfriend, I couldn't believe it! I thought she'd been lying! There you were in your black rhino skin trousers, your orange shirt and long pinstriped jacket, striding over in your boots looking a million dollars! Then you taught me how to roll my first cigarette, no one had ever taken the time to show me before you did'. She had an excellent way of building you up. There was something in the back of my head at the very beginning, something I wasn't comfortable within my gut but I had lost my ability to know what it was. I believed it was me. She told me it was me; that I was closed and emotionless. It was true. After my ex I had totally shut down, but the nightmares continued. Even after I moved in with my now current girlfriend, the nightmares continued. Then, at times, I started to find my girlfriend to be very stressful to live with, especially when she was stressed. She seemed to need constant validation. She was hard work to please. Despite this, our relationship moved forward. We bought a house together, we got married and we planned to have children. We travelled a lot and had some wonderful experiences and adventures together: Austria, Spain, Thailand, Singapore, Tunisia, Turkey and Bulgaria, Romania and The Canary Islands. Once we were married however things started to go very downhill!

On our wedding day, as we were posing for the usual photographs, my new wife said to me, 'You're my wife now, you have to do as you're told'. I was mortified and speechless! Despite everything, I'm still a naturally stubborn bugger! I WILL NOT do as I'm told for anyone but my parents, teachers or bosses and most of all God. I don't mind being asked to do stuff but I'm not a mindless f***ing drone! We had been together for three years before our wedding and I thought I knew her well enough, but I started to see a totally different side to her, a side I did not like very much. I largely ignored it because she had an excellent way of manipulating situations to her own advantage and make you believe that she was acting in your best interests.

Things took a drastic turn for the worse six months after our marriage when my father became desperately ill. Knowing that my father was poorly, my wife booked us to go away for Christmas to go to Spain. I did not want to go obviously. I didn't want to leave my dad. I hated it and just wanted to come home. My poor dad had spent Christmas in hospital having platelet transfusions and I wasn't there to support my family…but as long as my wife was getting what she wanted! Shortly after we came home my dad was diagnosed with leukaemia. I won't go into the awful details but his first response upon being told the news was 'I'm leaving here in a pine box'. He had no fight left. Anyway, he got chemotherapy and was in remission! Yay!!! But no. One week later after the results he got pneumonia. He died peacefully on 25th February, 2008 with my mother, myself and my wife at his bedside. Cancer didn't kill him, pneumonia did.

My wife was a great support during that time and for that, I will always be truly grateful. Her support didn't last long though! Six weeks later, she was all 'Are you not over that yet!' She was a bit of a c***. Erm, no I'm not! My dad just passed away, there is NO getting over it. I was only twenty-eight.

Whilst my dad was lying there desperately ill in hospital, my wife had demanded to book a three-week travelling trip back packing around Thailand. I was horrified at the idea! I had been away whilst he was poorly over Christmas and I was NOT going to leave him now! But as usual she put contingency plans in place in the event, we needed to come home. The trip was booked for April, only eight weeks later. The trade-off was this: she got her dream holiday and I got a baby.

As, I wanted to have children of my own I caved. Long story short we did not have children together. My body would not co-operate. Eeee, I wonder why. She became increasingly controlling and manipulative. She had hit me once or twice already but denied doing it. Once she got made redundant from her job, she became increasingly violent and spiteful. She would punch me and kick me or throw me against walls and hold me by my throat. She knew every button in me to push to get an angry response, and accuse me of abusing her! I am a Roman Catholic, and I was raised to turn the other cheek. I never ever raised a hand back to her…my voice yes, but my hands no. I tried to give her everything she ever wanted to make her happy, but it was never enough. She was not getting my humanity or dignity!

Her violence and abuse increased the more frustrated she got, and I got the brunt of it. I didn't dare say no to her! I wasn't allowed to have my money, but she would buy all kinds of shoes, handbags, jewellery and clothes…and never wear or use them! If I wanted to buy a new book, I'd get told to just wait until the library had it! ERM no! But I became terrified of her as her rage increased. She hit me one night in an argument because I was completing a task without her, and she had wanted to control it herself. I hadn't needed her help! I'm perfectly capable! I left the house without speaking to her, and she rang me on my lunch hour asking why she hadn't heard from me. Well, 'Because you hit me' I spat back. Her angry response, 'You made me do it; you should have just done as you were told!' I told her she was an abuser, which she did not take well.

I wasn't looking forward to going home to her! And yet another row ensued. I told her that if she ever hit me again or raised a hand to me, I would divorce her. She laughed in my face. OOOOO that wound me up, but I stayed calm and replied, 'And why not?' She laughed again and said, 'You're a Catholic; it's a sin to divorce. You'll never divorce me and besides it'll cost you and you can't afford it.'

I was prepared to save our marriage and I begged her to go to therapy, but no, there was nothing wrong with her. I have absolutely no doubt at all that a psychiatrist would have diagnosed Narcissistic Personality Disorder in her with psychotic tendencies. But she became more dangerous and did in fact attack me several times again. She tried to force me to go away for a spa weekend with her mother and sister (my worst nightmare as her mother is a narcissist too, although her sister is lovely). She wanted to take the car. I refused to go. It snowed heavily though, and the car was unable to go anywhere. But she was adamant about taking the car. I said, I needed it for work. She argued that she needed it to travel. Although I was afraid of her, I didn't want to see her get hurt trying to get the car out or drive such a long distance in blizzards (especially when she was such a lunatic driver to start with!) I told her she couldn't have the car. She screamed that if I took it, she would phone the police and tell them I had stolen it. I burst out laughing and giggled, 'Good luck with that, I'm the registered owner and keeper! You can't tell the police I've stolen my own car!' She was apoplectic with rage and threw the recliner at me as I walked out the door and buggered off to the pub.

As I sat in the pub on my own, I pondered and remembered my teacher training: never give an argument to solve an argument in an angry situation, basically because you'll just go around in circles arguing over nothing in the end, getting angrier and more frustrated. I had forgotten how to ignore and walk away from a bully, like I had as a child. I had become angry, and she knew damn well how to get it out of me. I had a personal epiphany that night. She went away for the weekend, and I did what I always do when I am troubled. I went to see my mam.

You must understand how much I adore my mother. We have a unique bond. I worship her and I am fiercely protective over her as much as she is over me. When I told her I was getting a divorce, and that I had taken enough she was very supportive. She asked if we could sort it like always before, and she would support whatever I chose as it was my decision, but I assured her it wasn't possible this time around. I told her everything my wife had done and fessed up completely. My mam had no idea this was going on, nobody did. Yes, she'd had her own run-ins with my wife…as had everybody at some point or other, but this was different. I told my mam that I was afraid my wife would kill me. I believed fully that she was entirely capable of murder and say I deserved it. Nothing was her fault. My mam was enraged…understandably!

So, I filed for divorce and made my wife leave. She hated that I would not engage in conversation with her about divorce finances. She wanted ten grand from me. Oh, she wasn't getting that! She had taken a job at the post office working nights until she moved out (still spending MY money! She hadn't contributed to the home in six months!) I finally had the upper hand and control of my own self. It infuriated her.

I came home from work one day; I had been delayed by snow drifts so was later in returning than usual and found her sitting in the recliner. Usually, she would be getting ready to leave for work, and we wouldn't really speak other than to be polite, but she was hunched over in the chair. I said, 'Hi' to be polite and got no response so carried on walking and glanced over at her. Then I caught a flash of red. I doubled back, concerned. She was sitting over a blood-filled bowl, covered in blood and surrounded by bloody tissues. I was horrified! She looked awful! She was holding a tissue over her nose and having a severe nosebleed (she used to get them). Long story short, I ran to get a warm wet sponge, an ice pack, more tissue and cleaned up the bloody mess. I tidied her up; her face and hands were covered in blood. She had a severe throat infection and could barely speak. I demanded that she see her GP as soon as possible. She didn't have the number for work, so I drove there through further snow drifts to tell them she was sick, and then I went to the shops to get her the ice cream she had asked for because she could barely eat. I got her some medication to help and then ran her a bath when I got home.

I was sitting in the armchair reading when she came out of the bath. She sat on the sofa diagonally opposite me. She humbly said, 'Thank you for helping me.' I replied, 'You're still my wife and I still care.' She asked if we could talk. I agreed. I wasn't sure what to expect; maybe an apology, a repentance? But she came out with 'Can we talk about the ten grand you have to give me when I leave?' I closed my book, stood up and replied calmly 'Nah, I don't think so. Good night!' I didn't owe her anything. The more I refused to discuss it, the angrier she got. And it p***ed her off that I would no longer engage in an argument with her. She had NO way of manipulating me into what she wanted. She hated that I had power over her and that I didn't need her anymore. Well tough f***ING titty!

My head was a total mess after she left. I had been in an abusive relationship twice now! What the hell was wrong with me? I went to psycho-therapy (not counselling). I went to a head shrinker, as if my head wasn't tiny enough already! I learned a lot about myself though and rediscovered the old Rachel and her old identity.

I had been having issues getting bullied at work by my bosses (I was not the only one!) and so, I eventually left, cracking under pressure and stress in 2012. I suffer from Fibromyalgia, diagnosed in 2006. My doctor had wanted me to medically retire. I laughed in his face and said, 'Then do what? Sit on my arse whinging? I think not! Tell me how to manage it and I will bloody well live it!' And so, I bloody well did! Mega stress is really bad though and I totally relapsed! It was awful. I hadn't fully recovered when I took on a new job that had me working fourteen to seventeen hours a day. I couldn't cope and was exhausted to the point I almost crashed my car.

In February 2012 I had gotten a puppy. I had always wanted another dog since Bruno, my first ever dog, but my wife had forbidden it. I wanted to raise him right, train him, teach him, work him and have his friendship and company. The job I had promised he could come with me as I wanted to train him as a P.A.T dog. It turned out that I was unable to take him along with me. He was only five months old. Neither did he have the qualities required to be a P.A.T dog. On one occasion I was forced to leave him for a long time on his own. When I got home, I cried, cried, and cried. Mason was my life. He didn't deserve that.

Eventually, I collapsed at work with a horrific relapse. I was exhausted beyond belief! I spent weeks on the couch unable to move. As always I had an excellent support network to get me through it all. I am truly blessed.

During my recovery I recalled a job offer I had been made. I had been in the dog park with Mason, my then four-month-old black Labrador puppy. He was bloody hard work! But I was determined to get him right. He was dominant, challenging and a biter. He was awful! But I wanted to understand him and fulfil his breed needs. I read everything, watched videos, studied him, monitored him, scrutinised him, corrected him, (never punished!!!) I quickly realised that dogs don't speak human because he seriously pushed boundaries (I still have the scars from the time. The little git split my head open!) and didn't listen to me. The more attention I paid to how a dog operates, the more I learned. And I had to learn how to speak 'dog'. It wasn't Mason that needed help; it was me!!!

So back to the job offer! I took Mason to the dog park, and he started pulling on the lead and bouncing like a loony, which is unacceptable. A calm dog is a happy and balanced dog, and so he had to learn to wait and calm down. I made him sit (you don't ask a dog, you tell it during regular training until it becomes a natural habit). He sat and waited, and I did not allow him to pull or take the dominant lead into the pen. Most owners would just release their dogs to go mental without checking the surroundings, the people, any obstacles, behaviour of the other dogs etc. but not me. I lead Mason into the pen as his friends ran over, and I made him sit and calm down. He was released only when he gave me appropriate eye contact. Even with the lead off he had to sit and wait until I told him it was ok for him to play with his friends. He was going to learn who was more dominant than he!

Once he was off playing with his friends, my friend shouted me over. There was a lady who wanted to talk to me. She was sitting with her friend, and her small handsome boy in a pram. She had three dogs with her; two beautiful Whippets, and a gorgeous tiny Griffin. I was a tad bewildered. I wandered over, still with an eye on Mason. My friend introduced us. The lady told me she liked the way I handled my dog. I naturally thanked her. She said she could use

40

someone like me. I hadn't a clue what she was on about. Her friend chipped in and said, she had a dog walking business. I thought it was excellent. The lady began to explain about her work. I was very interested. She said, she could really use someone like me. I was still a tad bewildered (I was still in relapse at the time and a bit slow on the uptake!) She could see I was lost but didn't make me feel awkward about it. She said, 'If you ever want a job working and training dogs just let me know. Are you working already?' I had to apologise and turn her down, as I was already starting a new job soon. Turning her down was a big mistake! I entered a job that nearly killed me!

During my second relapse, as I was recovering, I recalled the lady's job offer. I hadn't been able to shake it off. So on the off chance I emailed her to ask if the offer was still open. It was. We spoke over the phone and I was formally interviewed in the field with her. I absolutely loved it!!! The dogs were incredible, she was incredible and the locations were beautiful. She virtually hired me on the spot. She asked if I wanted to go out with her again. I jumped at the chance! I got fully involved from day one. I loved it and still do!

I am now a fully qualified Dog Psychologist, amongst my many other qualifications. I was given a quirky nickname by my brother after I started the job working with dogs. Over Sunday lunch one day, my family were commenting on how I was a changed woman since working with dogs. My brother laughed and said something along the lines of 'You remind me of Romulus and Remus'. I responded with 'Why?' and he replied, 'Cos you're like the She-Wolf that raised them!' and then he burst out laughing! And so the nickname stuck and I became Rachel She-Wolf BIRKBECK. Even my boss calls me the She-Wolf!

I am Rachel She-Wolf BIRKBECK BA (Hons) CG, Dip HE, Dog Psychologist. So this is me, my background, my starting place to this new journey that I am travelling though. I experienced a mixture of positive and negative experiences, just like we all do. Through my faith, I understood that these were learning curves towards what is ultimately more important; love and positivity. Never lose faith, hope or charity as these are our greatest gifts to ourselves and each other. I found this to be true. The bully who tortured my friend at school was just a soul in need and when we helped her, she became our friend. My first partner was damaged beyond my help and she couldn't help herself. No one can help such a person; they have to do it themselves. To be healed you have to want to be healed and want it with all your heart and soul. It means being honest with yourself and for some, that's too terrifying to face. It's heart-breaking. I pray for her every day, even after eighteen years of almost no contact. I used to light candles at church and pray for her happiness. She deserves to be happy just like the rest of us no matter how she behaved towards me. That was forgiven a long time ago. Turn the other cheek and forgive your brother or sister. What she did matters not now and I do not blame her or slander her name. I understand her better now, even though we have barely spoken over the years. We sometimes spoke about the children and I informed her when my dad passed over, as the children had adored him, especially the youngest daughter. She and the children were truly lovely and supportive and for that I am very grateful.

When her own mother passed over, she rang me to inform me. She was hysterical on the other end of the phone. I was immediately worried. I had great respect and love for her mother and my ex knew that. I got on well with her mam. She was funny, spiritual and loving; a quirky character indeed. I was devastated to hear the news of her passing and to hear my ex so wounded. She had phoned out of courtesy like I had her with my own father. I was unfortunately too ill with flu to attend her funeral. Upon hearing the news, I immediately sent flowers, despite what my wife thought! Strangely it was the only time, I could spend money on someone that wasn't her, but then it wasn't that strange when she went around telling everyone how nice she'd been letting me send flowers to my ex and on a glory hunt!

My journey through my marriage was meant to be. It was a lesson. I just had to learn to listen to myself again and regain control of my own self. My psychiatrist told me that I had NO identity that didn't belong to my wife. She asked me who I was. Every single thought or action had my wife at the beginning, or end of it. It was terrifying to realise that I was not me anymore! I was my wife's sub-self! I had no idea who I was anymore!

I went on a journey of self-discovery and tried to shake of my ex-wife's hold. It took a long time, as these things do. I was seriously damaged. My life had fallen apart yet again. But I had faith. Jesus said, 'I will tear down this temple and in three days rebuild it'. I could be rebuilt. I had a lot of love and support through it all.

I knew that my marriage was a trial I had to experience. There was a lesson there to be learned. When we make a mistake, it is usually because God wants us to reflect upon how we can change ourselves to become better people and not repeat the mistake. I had done it twice. I was not going to do it again. I didn't listen to my gut all the way through my relationship with my ex-wife. I was given warning signals multiple times, but I did not trust myself to listen to them anymore, until the end when I finally had my epiphany. God wanted me to realise that my ex-wife was beyond saving and beyond anyone's help. He wanted me to re-discover myself and the person I had been all those years ago; the confident one who trusted herself and her instincts and her spirituality. I had never trusted God; I had just not fully understood my role. But now I get it all.

I do not hate my ex-wife. She is now irrelevant to me. I realised a long time ago that her manipulative games no longer have a hold over me. Everything she says or does has an ulterior self-serving motive. Everything about her is false, and she is a chameleon who fits into any role that benefits her needs at any given time. She is a dangerous woman and I refuse to have any contact with her. To be honest, memories of her terrify me still sometimes. But I still cannot hate her. I don't hate people. That's just the way she is; completely inhuman and selfish. She has no control over that, which makes her dangerous because she doesn't accept that there is anything abnormal about her. And, so I refuse to have contact of any sort for my own sanity and safety. I am unhappy to say that I believe she is too dangerous to society as to warrant being behind bars after how she treated me (and others before me it turns out). But apparently she is not.

I learned valuable lessons from these experiences and I'm still learning. Never stop learning! When you learn you grow! I learned how to trust myself again. I learned how to be confident and stand up for myself. I learned how to walk away from bullies again. I learned how recognise a threat and manage it. I learned how to control myself again, manage difficulties and control a situation and how to let go of negativity. I wanted a life of calm and positivity. And I was going to have it!

My greatest teacher and support was Mason, my dog. He taught me everything I know about dogs and myself. I became a parent again. I realised that dogs need more than just 'ownership'. They needed a mother and a teacher to help them live in a human world that is unnatural to them. And it is in this dog-related world that we now begin the next part of our journey.

My point to all this background is that we can CHOOSE to either face adversity with positivity or negativity in our hearts. My point is that I became so wounded, I chose a negative path which led me to more unhappiness and negativity. I began to recognise that with the help of Mason. We grew together and now have a special and unbreakable bond. My family and friends were central in supporting my positivity too, especially my mother and Clare from school. I started correcting many wrongs and repenting of any sin I had committed in my ex-wife's name (she had offended many!) I regained old friendships, made new ones and found myself again. I regained the positive and my confidence. I became the She-Wolf and live by prayer, faith, hope, charity and love.

So, let us close this chapter with our opening prayer, as it is apt and fitting:

'God grant me the serenity to accept the things I cannot change, to change the things that I can and the wisdom to know the difference'. Amen.

Chapter Two

I am by far one of the clumsiest people on the face of the Earth! I can fall over fresh air and make it look like art! I just seem to attract mischief upon myself! The number of ridiculous accidents I've had at work is unreal! I've cracked my head on tree branches, tripped over roots, fallen into ditches, got tangled up in long lines, stung by nettles, shredded by thorns, stung by wasps, fallen into pot holes, knocked over by the dogs and on one occasion, struck by a stray golf ball! I've broken ribs and gotten bloodied and bruised, but never beaten!

That is up until I had a bit more of a major and significant accident at work in January 2014. It was a totally freak accident and no one's fault, just one of those things! I was at our training field and it was absolutely pouring down with rain. A Staffordshire Bull Terrier I was working with got herself a little bit over excited with a Spaniel and she began to annoy him. She was a beautiful girl, but once she got fixated on playing, she was pretty determined and I could see that a fight was brewing the more she pestered the Spaniel and the more aggravated he became. She had stopped listening to me and was fast becoming a liability. So, I went to put her back on the lead. As I went to turn her collar around to find the D-ring she suddenly reared up in protest and my hand slid all the way under her wet leather collar, where I had just been holding it with my fingertips. She then darted around in a circle three times on her hind legs, still trying to go after the Spaniel. I couldn't free my hand. She struggled out of her collar, tightening it around my finger as I desperately tried to free my hand! Then I heard the snap and felt the sickening pain shoot through my finger. It sounded like gun shot. I fell to the ground face down in the wet mud screaming in agony with the collar now dangling from my wounded finger. The Staffie was still causing havoc with the Spaniel and I knew I had to stop her before more than just I was injured! I gathered every piece of fight in me to get up, put her collar back on and take her back to the van. How I did it with one hand I will never know! But my dogs come first. Then I took of my leather gloves and surveyed the damage while trying not to throw up. The middle finger of my left hand was mangled! The top half was pointing left and the bottom half was pointing right! I quickly spoke to my boss who said she thought it looked broken when she asked me for photographs and gave me first aid advice over the phone. She offered to come and get me and take my dog's home so that I could go to the hospital. I was mortified. I refused and said, I would manage. I was going to get my dogs home safely come hell or high water! It took me longer, but I did it.

One of my clients who is an Accident and Emergency doctor demanded to see me that evening at the hospital. She had seen my fingers gaffer taped with green electrical tape when I dropped her dog off and was horrified by what she saw. My hand had started turning a sort of blue/green colour! I was still covered in mud and looked a right sodding mess.

So I went to the hospital that night where I was informed that I had a severe spiral fracture. When the doctor showed me the X-ray I nearly fainted and blurted out 'Holy s***!' and then rapidly apologised for my obscenity! She looked at me and said, 'I always knew you we were pretty hard-core, but never realised just how hard-core until I saw that! How you continued to work for the next six hours with that type of injury is beyond me!' I replied that I had a responsibility to my dogs to get them home safely. They are defenceless animals in need of protection and my priority; I could sort myself out later. My injury wasn't going anywhere!

Long story short, I needed plastic surgery and two operations on my severed finger to stabilise the break (I now have three metal screws in my finger). I lost the use of my left hand, which was a total p***er because I'm left-handed! Obviously I was not allowed to go to work because I couldn't drive and had no grip function, let alone hold a dog lead. I was in a splint and sling for months and had to have extensive physiotherapy. I didn't seem to be making any progress with it and I admit I felt defeated. I loved my job and being away from my dogs destroyed me. I had no reason to get up in the morning. I became very depressed and I dare say suicidal. The smallest things easily frustrated me. I once rang my friend Debs in tears because a light bulb had blown in my chandelier and there was no way I could change it. She came straight to mine and changed it for me, offering to help with anything else. I told her that my cat Ravyn had pulled down the curtains in my bedroom, and I couldn't fix it on my own. So, she helped me to do that. We had a good laugh, and she really cheered me up. My mother and my friends were an excellent support. I couldn't have got through it without them.

I was desperate to go back to work, but my finger just wasn't co-operating it seemed, despite the work I was doing. The ligaments and tendons were just too damaged and my finger just would not bend! Then the physiotherapists gave me this new little contraption to slip over my hand and then something like a little sling shot to go over my finger that I could tighten to help stretch the tendons and ligaments into compliance, building up the time I was supposed to wear it and the level of stretch every twenty minutes for as long as I could bear. The aim was to start at five minutes given that my finger had refused to move at all!

It was horrifically painful. I fought back tears constantly as I inflicted the pain upon myself. But it was pain I needed to experience. There was no other choice. I either persevered or lost the use of my hand completely. I wanted to go back to work desperately and be with my dogs again. I have mentioned before how stubborn and defiant I am and when I set my mind to doing something, I bloody well do it!

As you can imagine I had a lot of time on my hands to ponder, pray and meditate. I recalled the little prayer: this was a situation I could change, so change it I would! I reflected upon the Parable of the Fig Tree that Jesus tells his disciples. If you don't remember the parable, it's basically about a fig tree that won't bear fruit. Cover it in manure says Jesus, until it does. So basically it is a euphemism for us as humans. We are the Fig Tree that can't grow. Basically what Jesus is saying, is that sometimes you have to get covered in s*** to grow and produce positivity. Getting covered in s*** isn't a punishment, it's a gift and a blessing. It's all about perspective. Jesus reassures us that there is a point to suffering and pain; it's how we deal with it and what we do as a result of it that matters. We either wither and die inside and become useless and hopeless to ourselves and others, or we grow, and we fight, and we use our experience to support and help others and change things for the better where we can. Even though I had felt defeated, I knew I had to recover, no matter what, even if it caused me to suffer in pain. I had been fighting Fibromyalgia for years and succeeding. A broken finger wasn't going to hold me down. I wanted to go back to work and if I had to be in pain to do it, then I would carry that Cross just like Jesus did and suffer for the greater good.

So I carried on with my little sling shot thingy-me-bob, increasing the time and the stretch every day, until I could start bending my finger on my own little by little. Two weeks later I could wear it at a full stretch for half an hour with virtually no pain. Each week the physiotherapists measured my progress and the success was incredible!

One evening my mother came over to visit me after I had been to the hospital. I escorted her down the stairs and held her hand with my damaged one and squeezed her hand (it was soft and gentle as my grip had not returned, but some movement had). She burst into tears saying 'I thought you'd never be able to hold my hand again!' I was proud of myself for working so hard and the first reward for that was to hold my mother's hand. You can't begin to imagine how special that was if you have never been unable to do it!

The next step was to regain as much grip function as I could. I was going back to work come hell or high water! I had to use grip putty several times a day and strengthen my hand. The damage had been extensive and I had been told that I would never regain 100% grip function or manual strength in my left hand. The surgery to implant the screws had left my finger numb and at the risk of arthritis and future pain. Fine! But I would get enough grip function to return to work.

Merely two weeks later it finally happened! I went to physiotherapy for my usual assessments and therapy. As she was faffing about with my hand, I asked the same question, I had asked every week: Can I go back to work yet? When she responded, 'I don't see why not, you have enough grip function to drive safely now' I burst into tears giving praise to God and her. The other patients and physiotherapists stood up and gave me a standing ovation, clapping with delight! I was incredibly moved! They had seen my tears and frustration over the weeks as I pushed and pushed myself and begged and begged them to let me go back to work. They hadn't failed to notice how much I love my job and how much my injury had wounded my soul, not just my hand. I suddenly realised that as much as I had been praying for them, they had been praying for me too. We had all been praying for each other in our own ways and wishing well on each other.

I practically floated home in a bubble of delight! I was still weeping with gratitude when I got home and phoned my boss. She was alarmed when she heard me crying, but I assured her they were happy tears and shouted with joy that I was coming back to work! We were both over the moon! As so, I went back to work! A month earlier than predicted!

I went to church and gave thanks to God. I gave thanks for all of the support I'd had from my family and friends and the staff at the hospital. I prayed for them all and for their happiness. They had done so much for me and kept me strong in my hour of need. I couldn't have done it without them. I will always be eternally grateful and indebted to them.

As much as I had started off in a place of negativity, pain and fear, I ended that particular journey in a place of positivity and hope. It was a personal disaster for me, and I was in crisis at the beginning. But knowing I could work to change it by changing my attitude and perspective made me realise that I was only as defeated as I accepted. And I did not accept defeat, even if I had to suffer in the meantime to succeed. Anything was possible through God.

I swore I would never feel so defeated again. There is a reason for everything. Suffering brings about growth. I remembered the Parable of the Fig Tree and realised that each time I got covered in s***, it was a blessing and a lesson to which to improve from for myself and for others. It was to be a great lesson in my current predicament.

Changing me was my biggest achievement I reckon. We can't really change much else if we are truly honest with ourselves. Sure we change our cars, our houses, our décor, our furniture etc. but these things are merely material things; little luxuries, not necessities. Taking care of ourselves and each other is what is necessary and a Commandment. Jesus implored us 'This is the greatest Commandment. Love one another as I have loved you'.

Jesus associated with and healed the sinner, societies 'failures', the outcast sick, women (who were second class citizens back then). He forgave those who struck him, beat him, spat on him, scourged him, rammed thorns into his head and nailed him to wood and killed him. When we really break it down, Jesus was telling us that hate begets hate and that even though our enemies may harm us, if we give back love, it removes their power over us (like me with my ex-wife. Once I turned the other cheek to her behaviour, I got the upper hand!) But if we give them back hate, they have yet another excuse to hate us back and so it goes on. Like Jesus said, 'An eye for an eye makes the world go blind'. But love begets love, that's a much better way to live! Peacefully and without hate!

The more we hate, the more we poison our souls with anger, jealousy, vengeance, frustration and all kinds of negativity. We stop focusing on our self-care and focus on our target of hate. We are harming ourselves with this attitude. But when we love, we focus on the positive, we reflect upon ourselves and how we can be better people to help ourselves and help others. We cleanse our souls with love, especially when we forgive or repent. We become much more considerate, compassionate, generous, sympathetic, empathetic and all kinds of positivity. We become more divine in nature. I think that's a much nicer way to live! Why be filled with hate when you can be filled with love? Why have a burger when you can have steak?

Choose love, choose life. Be the Fig Tree covered in s***. It won't harm you. Go out there and own your s***! Accept the things you cannot change and change the things that you can. Starting with YOU!

Chapter Three

So this was my view on challenges. No crisis need be a personal disaster. Nothing could be unresolved or sorted out with a bit of faith and hope and support. I still had problems to resolve because, well, that's just life. It doesn't have to be a major drama or the end of the world though. My faith got me through. I understood God's Word more and more. I would not be blinded by grief and despair like before, although being merely human I did have moments of weakness and at times it was difficult to maintain positivity in the face of adversity. But that's ok, it is normal and human. It's what we then do to sort it all out that matters. We either get back on our horses and fight on or get trampled beneath the cavalry. To be honest, although I love horses and have ridden them (with hilarious consequences!), I am a far better camel rider! I just seem to get camels for some reason. Riding them is like riding on the ocean when you know how to move and undulate with them. I can undulate! But my butt can't trot with a horse!

Anyway I digress slightly from my original point not to waver in the face of adversity as this was to be one of my greatest lessons. My Fig Tree was about to get buried in s***.

My work was still not without clumsy accidents; you know, the usual falling over roots, walking into branches, tripping over pot holes etc. The irony is, I was the one who designed and delivered the training on Health and Safety to our staff! I had experienced every accident in the book over the years! But then I was to have another accident. I won't call it life changing because it hasn't changed my life, but it is significant to subsequent events.

I was working on a van different to my own on a wet day. A smaller height van. I was returning a little dog to the top safety cage, standing on the bumper of the van to reach in. My wet boot slipped from the bumper, and I fell, smacking my right tit off the metal guard edge of the upper floor. I had been holding the metal cage door open as I fell and as I slipped, I gripped it harder in my right hand for support. I ended up slamming the metal bottom corner into the side of my boob and trapping it in the cage door. I ended up dangling tit-wise from the cage grappling for support.

It was obviously painful and bruised for a while. But then it remained painful. I checked and nothing seemed untoward…until a few months later, when I found a lump. I saw my GP as soon as possible.

I was afraid and embarrassed as she examined me semi-naked, I mean who wouldn't be! I just seemed to know in my soul what was wrong and that frightened me somewhat. But I trusted my doctor to do the best. She examined me and told me she was concerned and that she was referring me on Fast Track to the Breast Clinic immediately. She asked me to get dressed and sat me down, which I did. I knew what was coming. She said, 'You do know what this is don't you?' I replied that yes, I knew. She agreed that I already understood that. She sorted the paperwork and told me; we'd cope. I assured her that I would do whatever it took. I said, 'you know me doc, I'm stubborn and defiant and a bloody sore loser!' She laughed and completely agreed with me.

I was completely torn apart; not for me, but for the people who would be hurt, especially my mother. I just didn't know what to say to her! I can't bear to see my mother wounded or especially be the cause of it. I'm very protective over her. A small part of me was worried about me, but I was mostly worried for others, those that I loved and who loved me. They had already gotten me through so much. I did not want to be a cause for concern or worry for them. I also needed to gather my own thoughts before I could speak to anyone about it, especially my mother. I knew it was going to be hard and I had to find every ounce of fight in my being.

I prayed to God for strength and courage. He gave it to me. That night I had a dream. I dreamed that I wanted to follow my dad on his holidays (that's what my brother called it when he passed over). We got to the airport. He checked in and gave his passport and went through. I gave my passport. I was rejected. My passport was all wrong. They couldn't accept it. I argued. The man said, 'There's nothing I can do. You're not going with him' and shut the window on me. I watched my dad walk away through the barrier. He turned and said to me, 'Sorry darling, you can't come. Go home'. I had to walk away and go home. I woke up knowing I would be ok.

I had new-found strength with my dad. I wasn't f***ing going anywhere! But I had to meet God halfway; that's just the way it works! I went to the hospital on my own the next Wednesday for the mammograms, ultrasound and biopsies. I

57

didn't tell anyone anything: My boss Holly and colleague and friend Dan knew I was going to the hospital, but not why. First off I didn't want to worry anyone for nothing. Second, I didn't want someone I loved sitting there for hours on end worrying on their own while I had all of these investigations. To me it was pointless. I would say something when it was necessary to do so.

I complied with the staff and let them do whatever they needed to do, no matter how painful it was. I won't lie; having an already painful boob squished into a mammogram machine was far from pleasant, but my other boob was fine. The radiologist was lovely. She had an Eastern European accent and was Bulgarian. She was very supportive and I told her how much I loved Bulgaria. We shook hands when I left and I thanked her. When the ultrasound radiologist later put the cold gel on my breast for the ultrasound, I burst out laughing; I'm very ticklish! He explained everything as he went along: how he needed to take biopsies from three areas and insert marker tags, so they would know where they had biopsied previously. The biopsies were done under local anaesthetic. It was a bit like getting a 'Billy Stamper' on your tit. There was a slight pressure of something round, followed by a click and a tiny pin prick sensation. The only ones where I bit my tongue and braced myself was the lymph node biopsies. The needle had hit a nerve which affected my damaged right shoulder and make me feel a bit queasy when the pain shot into my neck (I had suffered severe whiplash in a car crash in 2009 and damaged the nerves in my shoulder). But otherwise it was bearable and necessary. There was a lovely nurse on the other side, and we talked about dogs and her young Labrador. She held my hand and supported me through the more painful aspects of the investigation. I can't say it was an entirely painless physical experience, but I had a good laugh with the staff and maintained my humour through it all. As always, my dogs kept me afloat. They always make me happy and relaxed talking about them. God is always with me so I knew I was perfectly protected. I've never had my boobs apologised to quite so much though. It was hilarious!

After I had experienced all of these tests and investigations, I was sent back to the waiting room to wait and see the consultant and breast nurse. I was actually very calm considering. I was patched up with three wound pads on my breast where they had taken multiple biopsies. I was very sore and swollen. But I was alright. I was eventually led into a side room with couches; not a clinical room. The looks on their faces as they walked in said it all (I'm a psychic empath and medium…but more of that later). I can read people. My heart skipped a beat and I felt butterflies in my stomach; a normal human response, but I fought it immediately. God was with me and so was my dad. Before they sat down, I said, 'It's not great news, is it?' They took seats in front of me and the consultant spoke. He explained that they had found abnormal cells in my breast, probably caused by the injury to my breast that I had experienced. The biopsies would be sent for further analysis as they suspected cancer. He wanted me in for an MRI the following Wednesday with an immediate visit to the Breast Clinic. I had blood tests before I left the hospital.

I still wondered how to tell my mother. That frightened me more than anything else. I couldn't bear to hurt her. I would do anything to protect my mother from anything. I love her. Love is too small a word for how much I adore her. She is my entire world and the last person I would ever want to hurt. She was wounded when I had my wisdom tooth out! She knows I'm terrified of dentists and kept me company and looked after me after my sedation. Eeee, I was off the wall after it. I didn't have clue what I was on about!

Anyway, I didn't want to hurt her, but I had to tell her. We had planned to watch The Greatest Showman together at some point and have a girly afternoon, so we arranged it for the Saturday before my MRI. She was buzzing about our girly afternoon and ready to get the drinks out. I told her to get a drink ready and to sit down because I needed to talk to her. It was the hardest conversation I have ever had I think. I tried my best not to be dramatic and panic her. I explained about the injury and how my GP had been concerned and sent me for tests. She was furious that I had gone to the hospital on my own (understandably) but, I explained all that reasoning. She asked me what they thought, and I admitted that they thought it was breast cancer. Her eyes filled with tears. My heart broke. I softly asked her not to cry. I knew I would be fine and explained how I felt and understood things. I was still worried; it was the not knowing. I'm an organised person with plans and routines and I currently didn't have a fight plan.

My mam obviously bollocked me for not saying anything to her about having tests, which to be fair I expected! She told me I wasn't allowed to watch The Greatest Showman! I put my pet-lip on. We watched the movie and I fell in love with it. It became my fight movie. We talked again afterwards and I reassured her that I would be ok. She was incredibly upset. I could see she was buckling inside but staying strong in front of me. I knew she is needed to out pour her worry and upset. There was nothing I could do about that. I didn't blame her for being concerned; she had lost her youngest sister and her husband, and even more recently, her eldest sister. Her reaction was natural to any loving and devoted mother. I did not want her to be concerned as I knew I would be fine.

The following Wednesday I had my MRI. My mother came with me, and we went straight to the Breast Clinic as required. I started to become agitated. I just wanted to know what was going on. I wasn't afraid of having cancer. I was afraid of the unknown. A little while later, we were invited into the examination room where the consultant wanted to examine my breast further. The way that the nurse who invited me out of the waiting room looked and sounded as she said, 'Rachel, your results are in, come through' spoke volumes. It was not a positive voice. I knew what to expect. My mam hadn't missed it either. I asked my mam to stay behind the curtain as I sat there on the examination table in a hospital gown waiting to be examined. She didn't need to see the poking and prodding that was about to take place. I'm not and never have been a prude, but there are just some things that are better left unseen, especially as I was still so black and blue from the investigations. It would not have been pleasant for her to see and I didn't want her to be wounded by that.

I had forgotten my Rosary so she gave me hers. I prayed with it in my hand as they examined me and did what they needed to do. Then they called my mother around once I was covered up. They told me I had breast cancer. I said, 'Okay, so?' I was calm and collected. My mam started to cry. I told her I was having none of that! I was going to be fine. I needed a mastectomy of my right breast and chemotherapy. I said, 'Okay let's do this'. They just looked at me as if I didn't comprehend what I had been told, open mouthed! My mam was a wreck, understandably! I was not going to be a wreck or a victim. I had been a victim before. Not now!!!

Before I left the examination room, they wanted to take pictures. I asked my mam to step behind the curtain again. I opened my gown and said, 'Do you just want the one boob or both?' The Breast Nurse got her camera ready and I laughed saying 'Go on, you might as well get both! Did you get my tattoos in?' as I grabbed my boobs and posed them for the camera. They were highly amused as my mother exclaimed from behind the curtain, 'Eeee, our Rach you can't say things like that!' I laughed and replied that I would say what I wanted; they were MY boobs to talk about!

My mother was still upset but the staff were incredibly reassuring, mostly with her and told her not to worry. My cancer was entire treatable even if it had taken itself off for a wander elsewhere. And again more blood tests needed because my sodium was low.

We walked back into the Breast Clinic waiting room with my mother crying. I was calm as f***. I felt awful for the women waiting with their family, friends, husbands or partners. What if they got crap news too? How would they cope? How would they feel? How did they feel seeing my mother crying? I was filled with love and compassion for them. I just wanted to hug them all and make it all better for them. I could sense their fear and pain.

On the way out of the hospital, my mam lost her s*** and started going on about how I was leaving my job, selling my house, getting rid of my pets and moving in with her and so on and so forth! I was horrified! I was indignant and replied that I would be doing NO such things. I was absolutely fine, going to work and my life was normal. No one was going to lose their s*** or be having negative wobbling fiascos! There was nothing to fuss about in my opinion. It was no major bloody disaster! I wasn't worried, so why should others be having a meltdown! Oh no! I was not having that!

We arrived home at my mam's house. I obviously wanted to tell my brother about what had gone on and my mam agreed to phone him and ask him to pop in after work. I asked her to be cool, calm and collected so as not to panic him. I popped to the loo when we got home and I just heard hysterical crying from the living room. I ran in to find my mam, hysterical, on the phone to my brother saying she had been at the hospital with me and could he come round later. He was immediately on his way in a panic! I went absolutely crazy! I berated her 'What the hell are you doing? What did you say that to him for?!' She said she hadn't said anything to him. I told her she had rung him hysterical about me and panicked him completely, hence he was immediately on his way over! What she did she expect? My brother must have been worried sick!

My brother works nearby so he was there a few minutes later and found me on the back stairs getting some fresh air. He saw me and relief washed over his face. Looking as ever like our dad, he strode up the stairs and said, 'What's up with you now sis? You okay?' I invited him inside and my mam started to fill with tears again. I told her to stop it! I put my hand on his chest and started, saying 'Look bruv, I've been to the hospital for tests and stuff and I have breast cancer, but I'm honestly fine!' My mam started to cry again. My bruv being my bruv berated my mother laughing and saying 'Is that all? For God's sake it's one of the most treatable cancers! I thought she was about to pop her clogs when you rang! Get a grip! She'll be fine!' I thanked him for his support. He's a funny, deep and loving man is my brother. He said with a smile as he was leaving 'Just make sure when they rebuild it, ask them to make them bigger…and then use them!' I burst out laughing. Only my brother!

My sister-in-law and niece then came to my mam's. They were incredibly supportive and positive. My sister-in-law laughed and said, 'Trust our Rachel! If there's anything to have, she'll sodding have it!' Like I said before, I have a tendency to attract mischief! I laughed too and said, 'Well that's just me. I apparently don't like to miss out!'

We all had a canny good laugh together…especially about how I am not very good under sedation. I become a rambling and hilarious lunatic! One time after sedation, I had an argument with my wife about how they had stolen my feet and given me someone else's! Then burst into frantic tears because the nurse brought me Bourbon biscuits…which I hate! I won't describe the rest because I became hilariously offensive and used obscenities that are beyond my everyday speech, and it's quite embarrassing when I recall just how far out of my tiny mind I wandered!

My mam then took me home and she went off to see my granny and tell her. I needed to tell my boss. My boss was truly shocked. She had just thought my GP had over-reacted. My boss was covering my van for me that day while I was at the hospital. It was very kind of her. We spoke properly when she returned my van later on. I calmly explained about the chemotherapy and mastectomy. She just looked at me gobsmacked as I described my experience to her.

She had asked me how the MRI had gone; she knows I am very claustrophobic and suffer from anxiety from time to time. I had received two previous MRIs before, one on my head and one on my knee (I have Hoffa's Disease. That is one thing I cannot change so I just accept it and walk with a painful limp.) I described to her how this time had been a tad different! I was asked to change into a front opening gown. I had the cannula inserted for the contrast dye and lead to the machine, where I was asked to lie face down on the bed with my tits in what I could only picture as two egg cups! My boss burst out laughing! Only I could describe the experience in such a way! She asked after my mam and I told her that understandably my mam was upset and she just kept looking at me in this odd sort of way. I asked her why she was looking at me funny and she replied that I was just so calm it was unreal! She said she'd be melting down. I laughed and said, 'What is the point?' Panicking wasn't going to help anyone. I had already known in my soul what was wrong and she knew that. She trusted my instincts as much as I did. I had never been wrong about a sick dog, or my cat when she was sick. My boss agreed. She was still in shock that I was so calm about the news!

My mam phoned after she had visited my granny, her mother. I hadn't wanted my granny to be upset either and asked my mam how she was? My mam replied that she had been her usual selfish self. My granny had said, 'Eee, I don't know how much more I can take that this world throws at me!' Typically, my granny: oh, woe is her! Totally not supportive of my upset mother! Anyway, she had asked my mam if it was alright to phone me. My mam said yes to her but told her not to be a misery with me.

So later on my friend Clare arrived just as the granny rang. My granny started with 'Your mam came up and told me the news darling', then started to sing 'Always look on the bright side of life'. My mouth fell open and I said, 'You do know what the last verse of that song is don't you?' She replied, 'Eee, no, what?' I laughed and told her it was, 'Always look on the bright side of death!' She burst out laughing and apologised as I explained that it was from the Monty Python movie The Life of Brian and that they sang it as they were nailed to their crosses at the end! She hadn't seen the movie but had heard the song being sung at Butlins, without the last verse! Clare thought it was hilarious! My mam was incredulous when I told her! But that's my granny for you!

My two other friends, Debs and Jill came over that night too and were incredibly supportive despite their own shock. I assured them that I was fine and we had a good laugh. I went to work as usual the next day and had a blast with my colleague Dan, who is also a dear friend. She too was incredibly supportive. That night my boss rang me all in a panic, quizzing me about where my head was at and was I coming back to work. I laughed and told her I hadn't gone anywhere and what was she panicking for? She was worried that I wouldn't come back after surgery. I berated her for writing me off and panicking. I was going nowhere and couldn't understand why she thought I would. She had just wanted to know where my head was at because I was so calm and collected. I told her that if she was waiting for some sort of meltdown and breakdown, she was going to be waiting a long bloody time! She admitted that she had been expecting me to break. Nah! That wasn't going to happen! I had full faith in my recovery. I was not worried or afraid. It's not pleasant hearing that things in your body aren't co-operating, but we can either chose to grow in the s*** or be suffocated by it. I made a choice not to be suffocated. Cancer was not going to be who I was, as much as being gay is not who I am as a person, or having blue eyes, or my choice of tattoos, or the way I choose to wear my hair or clothes. Fibromyalgia is not who I am either and I've fought that for twenty years. I didn't rest on my laurels then and I refused point-blank to do it now!

At this point I would like to explain a little bit more about my faith and spirituality, so that you understand where I'm coming from, personally. What I'm about to tell you may sound odd, to some a little crazy and to some it may resonate with them. Chose how you feel about it. I described earlier that I am a psychic empath medium. Some of you may know what this means and some of you may not. That's ok, but I'll explain briefly. Being psychic means that you are able to commune with the higher elements of the divine; things beyond material understanding. It's instinctual and occurs in the soul. It's a strange gift of 'just knowing things'. It's not like the jokes 'Clairvoyant evening cancelled due to unforeseen circumstances', it doesn't work like that. Some folk get the gift of prophecy with that, some don't. Generally speaking, being psychic tells us what our souls NEED, not what our hearts WANT: it's not necessarily about being able to see into the future as this is a much rarer gift. Being an empath means you can feel other people's emotions as acutely as your own. It can be very painful and difficult to control, especially in large emotional crowds where the intensity can be overwhelming to even the most controlled empath. Being a medium means you can commune with souls who have crossed to the other side of life if they are able to communicate from the higher plains in some way. Some people seeking a medium to speak to a loved one are often disappointed when they don't come through and someone else steps forward for them. The communication is still a gift; your loved one may not be able to communicate yet as they may not be on the correct plain, or soul-healed enough, but a representative may well come through to pass on the message instead. It's a bit like someone else ringing you from their mobile phone because the person you want to speak to has no signal or laryngitis! Some souls communicate by moving things, knocking or tapping, sending scents you may recognise as them or they may appear in dreams, or a sensation on your skin. There are a multitude of personal ways they still watch over us when they can. We just need to recognise it as them and thank them for their love. There is no hatred, just love and peace on the other side of life from our crossed over loved ones. Some folk find these communications rather disturbing and would rather ignore them. But I view them as gifts, even if I don't understand their meaning at the time. We have to understand that the concept of time on the other side of life is totally different to that of the material world. And only later does a message make sense at the appointed divine time that it is needed to be understood.

I had one such experience that did not make sense at the time. I wasn't getting many hours at work so one afternoon; I was sitting in my study doing some preparation for my next days' lessons. I had left the adjoining doors open so that I could see from the study all of the way through the living room, dining room and kitchen. It was February 2012, not long before I was due to bring my little puppy Mason home, so it was just me at home with my little cat Chase who was asleep on the sofa. I'd left the doors open so that she could come and find me if she needed to. My back had started to ache as I was sitting working at my computer, so I decided upon a cup of coffee and a hot water bottle. I wandered myself off and sorted out both and went back to my work. A short time later I wondered why my back was still aching! I had forgotten to bring my hot water bottle in! I'd put it down on the sofa as I put my fluffy bathrobe on (a draft comes into my study). I walked into the living room to retrieve it and stopped suddenly in my tracks. Right there in the middle of the living room floor was a random conker…yes, a conker! It hadn't been there ten minutes before! And the doors were all open. I wondered if the cat had found it and played with it, but she was still asleep on sofa and hadn't moved and because the doors were all open, I would have seen and heard her playing only six feet away from my study with a little conker on a wooden floor. Had I dislodged a random conker from somewhere and not noticed? Hardly, I reckoned; I would have heard it dropping or rolling onto the laminate. I quizzed and quizzed myself with this random conker in my hand for the next half hour. I couldn't find an explanation no matter which way I looked at it. Had I even had conkers in the house? I searched top to bottom, even my car and found no other conkers anywhere! My mam and I would usually take my niece conker hunting in the park every autumn, but not that autumn as my mother had suffered an horrific injury while camping. She had slipped on a tree root, fractured her leg at the top and smashed her ankle badly in two places. She needed to have her ankle pinned and was in plaster for three months and then a splint boot (often referred to as a 'moon boot'). She was virtually immobile for the first three months because the swelling alone was horrific and she needed constant elevation. If she needed to go anywhere, it was in a wheelchair with a leg elevation. So that ruled out the providence of the random conker too!

I had NO idea where it had come from. I couldn't explain it at all. I held it in my hand in silence for a long time. Then I heard my dad's voice resounding in my head through the silence. He said in earnest 'Not conker…conquer!' I asked him what he meant. He replied vehemently 'You shall conquer!' I had no idea what he meant but I never forgot it and kept my little conker as a gift.

That night I had a dream, rather a bit of a nightmare really. I've never been afraid of dogs or animals, but in this dream, I was in a clearing surrounded by trees and shrubs at the perimeter of it. It was pitch dark and scary. A small pack of aggressive mongrels surrounded me from a distance. I knew not to run and become a moving target, so I stood my ground. They got more aggressive and snarling the closer they got to me. I became more worried and afraid the closer they got. They seemed intent on attack, despite the smallness of the pack. I still stood my ground. Then I heard a sudden pounding behind me and as I turned, I saw dozens and dozens of snarling black wolves bolting towards me over a hill top with a fury I'd never seen. I stared in astonishment, not fear. I turned to look at the mongrels who had started to back away from me. I realised the wolves weren't coming for me. They were coming for the mongrels. As the wolves rushed past me, they chased the mongrels into the darkness and I heard shrieks, screams and howling from the mongrels. I stood rooted to the spot, unable to move. A short time later, the wolves came out and surrounded me and escorted me to safety out of the darkness.

I had no idea what any of this meant at the time! A year later I had the Chi-Ro symbol tattooed on my left leg – that is the intertwined XP Christian symbol. It was seen by Constantine the Great in a vision and had his soldiers paint it on their shields (so the legend goes). It was given to him with the message, 'By this sign you shall conquer'. He won his battle.

My little conker had always been kept on my bedside cabinet until one day it disappeared. I assumed that one of my cats had found it (I now have four cats and two dogs), played with it and lost it. I knew it was still in the house protecting me and it would re-surface eventually. I had however never seen any of my cats' faffing about with my little conker. But I just knew it was still in the house somewhere as my cats are house cats (my house is very large!)

Then my mother's cousin was getting ordained into the Permanent Diaconate in the Roman Catholic Church and becoming a Reverend Deacon. It was to be a glorious occasion and a great family honour. I was going to be suited and booted and looking my very best for him! On the day of his ordination, I went to put on my best dress shoes. I hadn't worn them since my eldest aunts' funeral nine months before. I slipped my foot in and wondered what the hell was in the toe of my shoe! I tipped my shoe and out rolled my missing little conker! How on earth had it gotten in there? It had been missing for four years! Then suddenly turns up in a shoe I hadn't worn in nine months? On the day of a family ordination? It was a Holy sign. I returned my little conker to its rightful place at my bedside.

Just four weeks later my GP was sending me for tests because she suspected breast cancer. Although I was initially in a little cloud of human panic, I looked at my little conker that night when I went to bed. I finally understood what my dad had been trying to tell me six years before: 'By this sign you shall conquer'. I trusted my dad on this side of life when I was still able to hold him tight and breathe in his aftershave and strength. I trust him even more on the other side. Spirits can't lie in their place of love and peace. I had the airport/passport dream that night. Panic over!

Let me briefly explain something else as to why I trust my dad on the other side. In September 2011, on a Sunday, I went with my brother to get his tattoo, with a mind to getting mine done too. My first ones. I wanted the Alpha and Omega symbols on my wrists and so I got them. It was the day before my mam was to go on her first camping trip with her new partner. Later on as I was dropping off to sleep, my dad came through to me. I greeted him and he said he liked my tattoos very much. I'd been worried about my mother going camping and asked him if she'd be alright. He laughed and said, 'Sort of!' The next day on my way home from work I got a barrage of texts about how my mam was injured, her leg was broken, it was bad and she was coming home. I raced to my mam's like a loony to wait for her arrival. She eventually arrived home in what can only be described as a back to front cricket splint coming up over the knee. She was drowsy from pain medication and her partner was so upset. He had taken excellent care of her but my mam had just wanted to come home for treatment. I understood what my dad had meant with his 'sort of' comment. Luckily my mam was not put off camping!

So there you go, that's the background to my faith in my recovery. The next stage was to have a CT Scan as they wanted to see if the 'mongrels' (as I was now calling it) had taken themselves off anywhere else. In the meantime my consultant wanted to see me because my sodium levels were low. So, I went to the Breast Clinic with my lovely stepdaughter because my mam had a physiotherapy appointment and didn't want me to go alone. My beloved aunt had offered to come with me, having experienced a breast cancer scare herself, but she had just come back from a cruise and waiting to go on holiday again. She had worked hard for these things and I didn't want to intrude on her happiness or bring back negative memories for her.

My consultant told me that the mongrels had mildly spread to my ribs around my afflicted breast. He was worried about my sodium levels too and my kidneys. I described my diet to him and that when I calculated my sodium intake, I virtually didn't have any. I'd been diagnosed with a severe wheat allergy the year previously and lived a very cautious diet. He was not convinced. My bloods three years previously had been normal, but had been taken on a normal diet after I'd stuffed my face all day! When I had his lots of blood done, I hadn't eaten since the night before on either occasion. I know he's the doctor, but in my opinion, you can't regulate what you are not in-putting into your body! Sometimes your body does not regulate without help, especially if your diet is prohibitive, like a diabetic or vegan diet. If you don't in-put what it needs it can't regulate. Vegans and vegetarians often suffer with lack of protein and calcium which especially affects their feet. I believe I was similar having a severe wheat allergy and needing a strictly controlled diet. I was making myself ill through lack of understanding. And that was my failure to myself. But it could be corrected. *Change the things that you can.* I discussed the issue with my colleague Dan to whom I am close. We started Operation Sodium! I have been monitoring my sodium ever since and feel great. I can feel when it drops too low because I get a bit queasy. The consultant told me that low sodium could lead to seizures and fits and to come straight to A and E if that happened or I was found on the floor. Understandably I wish that not to occur! So I have kept a close eye on things. When I had a third lot of bloods taken that evening, I had eaten and stuffed my salty face in the hope that my bloods would be normal this time.

Before I left the hospital, the Breast Nurse wished to speak to me about treatment. I have two types of mongrels which are responsive to the newest treatments available, whether they have wandered themselves off or not. She did not want me to worry but had an air of concern about her. It was her natural 'nurse mode' of being, working with distraught women on a daily basis. It must take its toll on the soul coping with other peoples' upset. I got the feeling that she wasn't quite used to dealing with someone who was quite the opposite! When she'd told me about the two types of mongrels I turned to my step-daughter and announced 'I always knew I was special! I don't do things by halves like. I've got titty twins!' My step-daughter burst out laughing. The nurse really had no idea what to say to that. She must have thought I was crazy! She just looked at me with complete astonishment, as if I didn't understand what was going on. She reiterated that I was entirely treatable. I understood completely. She asked if I had any questions. I said I did.

I had been sent information and been asked to take part in a clinical research trial called 'Horizons', which was about supporting folk with certain types of mongrels. I asked the nurse about it because I wasn't quite sure how to fill it in, as I hadn't started treatment or anything. I wanted to help. As a trained historian and very nosy researcher myself, I feel it is imperative to support research, studies and teaching for the benefit of the greater good. During any treatments I have had in the past and been asked if students can be present, I have always agreed. They need to start somewhere and we should support their learning…they are our future scientists and healers. To deny them is selfish. She explained it to me. Everyone with a diagnosis like mine was sent the information as each hospital has their own research team to feed into the programme. I felt I kind of knew that already, but she continued: she was pleased I had asked about it. I said, 'Oh!' She replied that they thought I was an excellent candidate for the programme and had hoped I would take part. I was actually shocked and asked why? She smiled and said, 'Because you are so calm and coping. You are the calmest patient to ever walk through our doors. We've had women run screaming through the doors hysterical upon diagnosis.' I looked at my step-daughter and back at the nurse saying that was so sad. I desperately wanted to help such frightened women. The nurse said she could put me in touch with the research team to help me fill it all out. I was very grateful.

My mam rang just as I got home from taking my step-daughter home. I explained everything to her about the mild spread but how it was treatable etc. I told her everything. It is a sin to lie and a Commandment not to lie 'Thou shall not bear false witness'. I am not going to lie to my own mother. The second Commandment is 'Thou shall honour thy mother and father'. I could be tortured before I would ever lie to my mam!

And never then! I assured her I was fine. My CT scan was for the next evening.

I had never had a CT before so had no idea what to expect! It was a full body and head scan for obvious reasons. I was bloody starving. I hadn't been allowed to eat for the previous four hours prior to the scan so I could have eaten a scabby donkey by that point. All I wanted was a kebab for some reason! So off I trotted into the room, with my mother in the waiting room. I gowned up and put my clothes in a little blue basket to take into the scanning room. As the radiologist was asking if I'd had a CT before I said, 'No' and that I was completely claustrophobic and suffered from motion sickness. He said the claustrophobia usually wasn't a problem for sufferers but the motion of the moving bed sometimes was. I had no idea what to expect. Then I walked into the scanning room and saw the largest Polo mint I've ever seen in my life! There was a bed positioned to go back and forth through it. A Polo with a giant hole-O! I found it quite hilarious! I was invited to lie on the bed while I was asked the usual questions. The only ones I could answer yes to were the ones about hay fever and allergies. I joked about how long this would take because I was clamming for a kebab. The radiologists, who were lovely, laughed. I jokingly asked if they did kebabs on the NHS. They said unfortunately not. I laughed along and said, 'Just imagine how many more women would come for a smear or mammogram if they were prescribed a kebab afterwards. It's a total travesty! Kebabs save lives!' We had a great giggle about my wheat allergy and how the machine looked like a donut. I couldn't cope with it being a donut; I love donuts but could no longer eat them! We laughed and laughed. The female nurse inserted the cannula and explained everything. And so we began.

The movement of the bed wasn't too bad. It was more a backwards and forwards gentle motion, much like undulating on a camel or floating on the waves...both sensations which I find pleasurable and calming. I had been asked to place my arms above my head. I closed my eyes and relaxed, actually finding it all to be rather cathartic, even though I was still starving and ready to eat the radiologist! And then it was done. The radiologist was lovely and asked if I wanted a minute to orient myself, knowing I got motion sick. I said I thought I was fine and sat up, feeling ok. I exclaimed 'Wow that was fun!' He looked at me with a quirky odd look. I said to him laughing, 'I bet you don't get many patients saying that to you!' Stunned, he replied open mouthed, 'Eeeerm no! But I'm glad it wasn't horrid for you!' I then had to wait for a while to make sure the contrast dye hadn't adversely affected me before the cannula came out and I could get dressed to go home. The nurse was lovely. I usually wear a cap when I can't be arsed to do my hair but had taken it off obviously. My first instinct after having the cannula removed was to put my cap back on so I reached over....to what was a round sick bowl next to me! I almost wore the bugger! That would have been a look and a half! The nurse and I laughed like crazy, having a good giggle about it.

Once I was dressed, I wandered out into the waiting room only forty minutes later where my mam had been chatting to the receptionist. I sauntered through the doors like 'Fanny-gis-a-bit' and announced that it had been fun! (There were a couple of surprised faces!) My mam asked if I was ok. I replied, 'Yip! Other than starved! I'm off for a kebab!' My mam turned to the receptionist, shrugged her shoulders and said, 'Told you!' The receptionist burst out laughing and bid us goodnight and we thanked her for her support.

My mam kindly took me home and bought me a kebab. I would have bought it myself but she wanted to make an offering. I realised a long time ago, that when someone who loves you offers you what you need, not only is it a gift to you, but also to them. Your acceptance is a sign that you respect their offering of love to you. We seem to have lost that gift to be grateful and respectful. We become stubborn and deny the help our souls really need, but are happy to accept the help that our hearts want. I needed a kebab (it is a salty food and I craved it for my sodium levels) my mam fulfilled that need for me. It was a great gift. Gifts come in all kinds of ways; we just need to be able to understand what we truly NEED, not what we want. I mean, what's more beneficial to a thirsty man; a glass of water or a bag of diamonds? The man who choses diamonds choses death. He doesn't need them, he wants them. And he rejects the water he needs. What use is a bag of diamonds to a dead man? Had he drank the water he NEEDED, he would have lived. He may not have had diamonds as a result of living, but in choosing them over the water, he wasted an opportunity to find out what he could have had.

There is a choice. I chose not to refer to my little blip as 'cancer'. I find it very negative. I'm not negative about it. I chose to see it in a more humorous light. I work with dogs and relate to dogs and dogs cheer me up. In talking to my friends and family, I refer to the 'c' word as mongrels when I recalled my dream about the mongrels and the wolves. I called my supporters and treatments the 'Pedigree Attack Dogs'. There are many more of those than the 'mongrels'. I am not afraid or worried. And this is where the title of this book comes from: *Mongrels versus Pedigrees*. For me, it's a much more relatable way to fight; a one filled with humour and positivity. You too must find a similar way to fight in whichever positive way resonates with you. It's not the end of the world and doesn't have to define you in any way. Like I said earlier, we are only limited by how far we are willing to accept defeat. And we have a choice. We are warriors together.

God grant us the serenity to accept the things we cannot change, to change the things that we can and the wisdom to know the difference. Amen.

'I come to you Lord for protection; never let me be defeated' Psalm 31 V1.

Chapter Four

I find that waiting is the hardest part; it's the not knowing. It always has been for me. Even when I was going through fertility treatment and there was a two-week wait after inseminations before I could test. Was I pregnant? Was I not? When you don't know you can't have a plan. When you want something as badly as a baby, you live with constant hope that it worked this time round. And when you need healing and are waiting for results, it's equally as hard...because you have time to fear. You have no plan. You have no fight tactic. You have contingencies but that is all these are until you truly find out what you are facing. They are a small consolation when you are waiting for larger news.

After my CT scan, I had another week to wait before I would know if the mongrels had spread any further than my ribs and into any internal organs. Although I was assured it was entirely treatable, the not knowing was a bother to my soul. I personally didn't feel like it had, as much as the consultant was concerned about my kidneys and had discussed referring me to an Endocrinologist. Yes, my sodium levels were ridiculously low, but I personally felt this was diet related and not mongrel related. So I was awaiting results on that too after my efforts to improve my sodium intake and diet. I didn't feel half as crap as I had! If I felt my sodium dropping for any reason; I hadn't eaten enough salty food, I had diluted my blood too much with coffee, water, juice or a beer, or I had sweated profusely at work etc. and lost fluids, this could be rectified. *Change the things that you can.* When my sodium dropped too low, I would feel nauseous and get horrific cramps, especially in my feet and legs. My wheat allergy too caused me to lose a lot of weight…and sodium. I felt weak and lethargic and didn't have half the bodily strength I used to! My consultant had argued that my diet wouldn't make a difference to my regulation and that even inputting more sodium would not make a difference, but like I said before, you can't regulate what you don't have! Since I have started monitoring my sodium, I have noticed a MASSIVE difference in my physical strength, my skin, my mood, my nausea and my appetite. I did find an incredibly helpful antidote to the nausea if my sodium levels ever dropped too low and I couldn't access salty food immediately, but it is not my place to discuss it on these pages. I believed I had started regaining weight since understanding my difficulties a lot more! My rings weren't falling off my fingers and I didn't have tin ribs any more. I had to loosen my shoe laces because my feet put weight on too…not swelling of any sort! It was genuine weight! I could feel my ass getting bigger as I sat down! I didn't feel as bony or as uncomfortable! My pain levels were slowly reducing because I wasn't over-compensating as much. I could sit a lot more comfortably! This was in the space of less than a fortnight now that I had started retaining proper nutrients! When I got weighed, I had in fact put on half a stone! I was jubilant! My stupid diseased knee was and is still an issue (there is nothing I can do about that) but at least I had more energy to drag it around now! In a roundabout way, my mongrel diagnosis had changed my life for the positive in other ways! I started to take better care of myself and understanding a lot more about my own personal needs.

I suppose in one way I had been in self-denial: I'm fine as I am! Obviously I was not fine. I had been losing weight and becoming more and more lethargic. I put it down to a progression in my Fibromyalgia and a prohibitive diet. I had issues to deal with already and didn't know what symptoms to attribute to what. And I took painkillers to cope with the Fibromyalgia pain. Had I masked other symptoms inadvertently? All these questions run through your head, but realistically you'll never really know. It's normal to question things. We wouldn't be human if we didn't. But we have to realise how pointless it is to scrutinise the inscrutable. All we do is torture ourselves without need. All we need to focus on is what is happening in the here and now. *What can we change and what do we need to accept?*

I reflected further upon my little prayer and realised that sometimes we actually need to compromise. Sometimes we need to accept something in order to change it. Two prime examples of which I discussed earlier on: my two abusive relationships. I could not accept they were a disaster. I believed I could genuinely love them enough to help them. I had to learn to accept that I could not in either situation and change my own behaviour in order to manage those situations. My first partner refused to accept her alcoholism and therefore could not change. My ex-wife could not accept she was psychologically damaged and therefore would not change. So I had to accept the situations and then change it. It wasn't easy, as I discussed.

I can't change the fact I have mongrels, but I could change my attitude towards it, my diet and how I chose to fight and support others through it too. Either become a fruit bearing fig or stay rooted in s***! You always have a choice: optimist or pessimist? Negative or positive? Glass full or half full?

Then I had an epiphany after a three-and-half-hour conversation with a dear friend from school called Rachael. She knew I had always been in love with one particular lady. Our relationship had been brief but deep and meaningful. We were a mutual match and made each other happy, or so, it seemed. The reasons it fell apart are not to be discussed on these pages but five years later I was still affected by it without realising it.

In living with her I had never known such mutual love and respect, such happiness and relaxation. We just 'got each other'. Everything was just so easy, mutual and compromised. Nothing was a problem when we were living with each other in our own private bubble. When we parted ways, it was difficult for both of us. I just didn't understand what had suddenly gone wrong. I lived in a very black and white world of 'if I love you and you love me what's the issue?', but her world was a lot more complicated than that. She didn't have the support that I did from the most important people. I had experienced a great deal of love and support and I just didn't understand people who had not shared a similar experience: not necessarily the person who had suffered, but the people who had not provided the support needed for that individual. I found it very sad.

I suppose I also hadn't realised how wounded I still was from two previously extremely abusive relationships and when I found true love, I had no idea how to deal with it when it collapsed in flames. I didn't know what to do. I didn't know if there was *anything* I could do! I became angry and frustrated and felt used. I still loved her deeply and intensely and always have. Anyway, I handled it all very immaturely and angrily with her. But I never ever stopped loving her.

When she left, I was so devastated I suppose I began living a half-life. I hadn't actually realised that until I spoke extensively to Rachael that night and then had my epiphany. My friends and family were a great support to me during that time. I cried a lot; much more than I ever had during my divorce. This time I was truly wounded rather than just angry and frustrated at myself for putting up with so much crap for so long. I stopped going out and socialising. I became depressed and reclusive, losing all self-confidence. I couldn't sleep. I couldn't eat. I pined for her like a lost puppy. I went from having the best fun ever in my life to complete and utter heart break in a short space of time. I still pine for her if I am honest. Then six months later I severed my finger at work and my life became a very dark place. I wonder if I hadn't been pining so badly for my lost love, I might have dealt with my injury better. I had lost the love of my life. I was not going to lose my beloved job! So where I couldn't fight for my love, I fought for my job instead and made that my fight.

I had been living less than a life really and become so used to it that I just hadn't realised. I live for work and that was about all really in terms of fun. I love my job and every day is a new challenge and adventure. It's far from boring and filled with a great amount of love. I couldn't imagine doing anything else now and I've supported myself in a variety of jobs from advertising, to retail, to catering, to customer service, to teaching, to care work and now finally as a Dog Psychologist. I found my niche in the world thanks to Mason and Holly. My mam always fills me with incredible joy whenever we see each other or speak to each other. Just the mere sound of her voice calms my soul like I'm speaking to God directly. I once quoted the movie The Crow in a Mother's Day card to her: *Mother is the name of God on the lips and hearts of all children.* A young child depends upon its mother for the gift of life, the nurturing, the teaching, the protection, the devotion and the love. Every young child initially sees their mother as their superhero. My mother remains my superhero and goddess. I might be nearly forty years old, but I am still my mothers' baby and I still appreciate her love and wisdom. She and my dad brought me up to be respectful, generous, compassionate, accepting, helpful, loving and to appreciate the value of everything we had. We were taught to learn and how to entertain ourselves. We weren't ever given things 'just to shut us up' or 'keep the peace'. We were appropriately disciplined if we stepped out of line. There were consequences for breaking the rules and appropriate discussions about our bad behaviour. We were forgiven but never given in to just for an 'easy life'. We weren't able to just stamp our feet long and hard enough and just 'get'! If we wanted it, we had to earn it in some way. My parents were and are incredibly generous people and we were often treated to various days out, movie nights with takeaways and lovely holidays abroad etc. I have incredible memories of childhood and beyond.

Having mongrels has made me realise that as an adult I feel like I have failed myself a lot, by not trusting my instincts. As a child, I trusted my own instincts and the love and wisdom I was given and nurtured with. Only when I stopped trusting my own soul as an adult did I start stop trusting myself.

Corinthians 13: 11-12: *When I was a child, my speech, feelings and thinking were all those of a child; now that I am an 'adult', I have no more use for childish ways.*

For me, this statement has several interpretations and meanings. The rest of the quote goes on to say how the writer sees things more clearly now as an adult (he understands the Word better, where he didn't as a child). It also expresses a transition from childhood to adulthood where we lose 'childish' behaviours and become more self-aware and take responsibility for ones' self rather than relying on others. This also does not mean, on the same hand, that we should lose our innocence and trust in our own souls, like a child does. Jesus Himself said, *'Let little children come to me, for theirs is the kingdom of heaven'.*

Children are innately innocent and without tarnish. They have trusting souls. They believe in what the rest of us can't see: fairies, ghosts and imaginary friends etc. These things are perfectly real to them until adults tell them repeatedly that they are not. I'm not saying that these things are, just merely that innocent children believe in the impossible and invisible until they are told otherwise repeatedly.

I've been interrogated many times about my faith in God and questioned extensively about 'why' I believe when there's no 'proof'. Some people just get it when you explain and some people just don't and some people just refuse. No matter how hard some people have tried to shake my faith and make me disbelieve, I physically CANNOT fail to cling to God. 'Hear oh Israel the Lord your God is one and you shall love the Lord your God with all your heart and soul'. For me, that is a statement of fact, not 'belief'. I cannot explain the unexplainable to a closed heart and mind. They do not understand the parables. They do not understand that God is always there for them; they just have to ask. Unfortunately, when some people ask, they ask for what they want, not what they need. Big difference! God always gives us what we need; but not necessarily what we want. When they are refused what they WANT, in the timescale they WANT it and are denied, they blame God and deny Him, rather than asking for the simple things they NEED and being patient and listening for His guidance: He communicates and offers gifts in many ways, where most people demand some sort of major miracle to 'prove' He has listened and responded. How many little chances for an answer do we miss because we are waiting for a bigger answer?

I'd like to give such an example of a teeny prayer being answered where God has listened to me and given me what I needed. It may seem insignificant to some, but not to me because it had been an issue that was troubling me.

My six-year-old female cat Ravyn toilets inappropriately. My house is full of clean litter trays but she is very parky and picky. She refuses to toilet in a tray that has been used (even once!) and refuses to toilet in front of any of my other pets. She took to toileting excessively in my front hallway to the extent she rotted my wood floors and wall. No matter what I did she seemed to find a way around it! I became increasingly frustrated, as did she. I did not want my cat to be unhappy! My hallway did not smell pleasant, as you can imagine! Her behaviour was not acceptable, but nothing seemed to solve it. I then decided to build a high gate to prevent ALL of the cats entering the hallway (I didn't want any of them scent marking on top of her mischiefs). It was awkward to get my dogs out, but it was fine as long as the cats weren't getting downstairs. This worked well until she learned how to get over it and so did my male cat Gibbs. It was infuriating. There was NO need for Ravyn to continue her behaviours. She would hold and hold and hold herself all day until I went to bed, then scale the gate and toilet all over the hallway just out of pure habit, even if I'd JUST changed her own toilet. I had to try and change her behaviour.

I thought of ways I could prevent her from getting over the gate and thought that a bit mesh on top might just do it. I pondered this for a few days, thinking how I could best change her and help her to see that she had other options. I thought a lot about the mesh solution. And wondered what type? How would I fit it to our best advantage? Where could I get something appropriate? How much would it cost etc.? And then I went to pick up two dogs at work. The client had a skip on her drive and as I walked by, I noticed the dismantled wired front of a discarded rabbit hutch lying there. The owner gave me permission to salvage it.

I refurbished it and fitted it to the gate with the help of my darling friend Clare. God had obviously answered what I had NEEDED, not what I had wanted. It may just be a small insignificant event to some because most folk ask for the larger things in life. At the time I asked, I need some mesh and God gave me it! It was unusable as it was and I had to work to get want I WANTED from the gift, but that is the whole point! I thanked Him and praised Him for his generosity. God gives us what we NEED; like I said before, we have to meet Him halfway. When we receive a gift, it is up to us to bring it to fruition to get what we WANT. We have to earn it. God gives us mustard seeds (the tiniest of all seeds!) Do we ignore them because they look insignificant and fruitless? Or do we plant them and watch mighty things grow and reap the rewards for our trust and patience? Too many people are given mustard seeds, the little things and then fail to plant them. Then they wonder why their plans don't come to fruition and blame God for not answering them. Planting takes time and nurturing and we have to do this ourselves. God gives us the seeds, even the tiniest ones, but it is up to us to take care of our little seeds that He gives us. We must be *'the seed that falls on fertile ground'*: Let us plant those tiny seeds and watch them grow into from what we NEED into what we WANT. Only then will we have truly earned what we want with an honest heart and soul and God will reward our faith in Him; but our reward with be greater in heaven. The other part of the deal is this: we are given fruit in order to bear fruit. So when our little seeds grow, we share those seeds with others. Not everyone accepts the gifts of those seeds because they are expecting something larger than a little seed; so when you share your experience of receiving the little seed, it is rejected as insignificant and the recipient of the intended seed allows it to die in their possession. Some plant it but are too impatient to wait for it to bear fruit and then others are content to plant it, nurture it, watch it grow and bear fruit. When we bear, we share! The Lord said, *'Go forth and multiply'*. This has been mistakenly interpreted in a reproductive sense of 'create a bigger population', when it actually means 'Go forth and bear the spiritual fruit of love, faith and peace' to enrich the planet. When we grow our little seeds, we must plant with love. The fruit they will bear are the seeds of love. It is up to the recipient of those seeds to continue planting and nurturing them. And so on; the cycle of love and peace that was intended. But unfaithful humans f*** it all up being greedy and spiteful, jealous and hateful and a multitude of other negative feelings that are unnecessary. But God gave us free will. He gives us the seeds. We can choose to accept them or not. To plant them or not, to nurture them or not and to distribute their fruit or not. It's easy to blame God for our failings when we have no one else to blame for our lack of self-direction. He gives us the tools, but we have to do our own DIY. We have to meet Him halfway.

The small gift of the mesh gave me a few invaluable lessons. I have understood the meaning of Scripture in a whole new light just by writing. It is a huge gift to me and I give praise and thanks to the Most High Jesus Christ for opening my eyes further. I hope to bear further fruit. This is my mission. To provide seeds for my fellow 'breast brethren'. You can save people, just with tiny seeds.

I have to give credit to an extremely spiritual and eloquent man named Roland for the illumination I received in the Parable of the Mustard Seed. I believe it is a beautiful and sweet story. We speak often, although he lives far away. He has been a great support and close family friend since my dad passed over to the other side of life. One day, he had been at Mass (I had broken my finger at the time) and he had been praying extensively for my healing. We had spoken a lot about faith, scripture and healing and the power of God's love during my recovery over the years since my dad had crossed over. As he was kneeling at Mass praying, he had looked down at the pew in front of him and saw six tiny mustard seeds randomly resting there. He sent them to me, glued into a card, where he had glued them into a smiley face arrangement complete with two red hearts for ears and a silver star for a nose. For my healing. The number six is significant to me in the numerology concerning the conker gift. Roland still calls me Mustard Seed to this day. I have since understood the parable and the gift in a deeper way during my prayers and meditation. It has been a true enlightenment for me. My family and I are honoured that he thinks so highly of us all; we think extremely highly of him too!

And so this is how I dealt with the notorious 'wait'. I pondered, I prayed, I reviewed scripture, I drew upon the enormous strength and faith of my family and friends, I examined myself and paid more attention to things *I could change* about myself in order to feel better and get fight-ready, no matter what the fight brought to the ring.

My kickboxing instructor once boomed, as we were getting fight ready and training hard, 'Don't enter a fight with any thought that you might not win. If you think that, you've already lost!' For some reason those words resonated with me. He was right though. If you feel defeated before you've begun the fight, what is the point in the fight itself? You are just getting beat up for nothing and gaining nothing from it, other than a truck load of injuries, wounds, bruises and lost blood without getting a single punch in. You just end up trying to defend yourself without ever facing the assault head on with every ounce of skill and creativity you have in you. You fight as many rounds as you need to, learning about your opponent and how to beat them each time. This is why fighters study each other's fights beforehand, to give them the best possible advantage, but the fight itself is where the real learning begins. So fight to win or don't bother to fight at all.

My instructor also advised us 'Never enter a fight with anger or vengeance in mind; you lose focus to rage and will lose. Enter the fight with peace and respect'. Again he was correct. I understood what he meant. Fighting needs focus and skill, not hatred or rage. It was almost as similar as Jesus saying 'Love your enemy'. As discussed previously, hate begets hate, but love begets love. Sow the correct seeds. Our goal should be to make our opponents love us, not hate us, even if they have had some reason to in the past. We have to give them a reason to forgive us…chuck them a little seed! We have to be a bigger, stronger and more loving fighter; but fighting for the correct things. If we fight for the wrong things (which I have done, we only get more of the same later). If we fight for love and win, our reward is more love! How wonderful is that? And fear begets fear. We allow the negative to rule us when there is so much positivity to be had!

If there is one thing in life that we truly do own, it is our selves. This is why life is a gift. It is the only gift that is truly ours; the rest is merely trifles and luxuries. We have free will. If we can't own ourselves, then we don't deserve to own anything else. The only thing we ultimately do have true control over is our own attitudes. Those are the things we can *change.* We don't always have to be someone we don't wish to be.

I kept busy during the 'wait' and to be honest not really worried by the end of the wait. Like I said before, I didn't feel like the mongrels had f***ed of anywhere else. I was eating like a horse, I felt perfectly well, I had gained half a stone, I had stopped feeling nauseous; I had stopped having cramps and excessive pain. I had made some alterations to my life and diet and I felt great. I discussed it with my mam and Dan. I refused to believe that the mongrels had wandered off anywhere nasty and causing a problem. I just knew it in my soul. I knew that whatever the result was though, I would face it in the same way; it could be challenged and dealt with. The night before I was due back to the Breast Clinic for the results of the CT scan and the bloods, I thought I might be worried, but I couldn't be. I did some writing, pondering and praying and some further meditating. I had found joy at work and had a good day with Dan and my dogs. It was filled with laughs and love.

I had an early night and set my alarm to get up for the hospital the next morning. I slept soundly and without worry. I knew the Lord was watching over me. I closed my eyes, listened to my music with my Rosary in my hand like I usually do and prayed to our Holy Mother like usual in my nightly meditations. I slept soundly and comfortably drifting off to the soundtrack from The Greatest Showman; a musical that had inspired me so much and allowed me to find meaning and expression for my feelings in having always felt 'different' in some way. I began to celebrate myself internally a lot more and take better care of myself. That movie was to be a turning point in my journey and attitude and I bless my mam for recognising that I would love it and eventually NEED it. I would also like to extend my deepest gratitude to the cast of the movie for inspiring me so much; particularly Hugh Jackman, Keela Settle and Zac Effron. The movie actually expresses the Parable of the Mustard Seed beautifully. Maybe that is why I appreciate it so much.

So let us end this chapter with the Parable of the Mustard Seed itself for our own prayer and reflection.

Matthew 13:31-32: *'Jesus told them another parable: The Kingdom of Heaven is like this. A man takes a mustard seed and sows it in his field. It is the smallest of all seeds, but when it grows up, it is the biggest of all plants. It becomes a tree, so that birds come and make their nests in its branches'.*

Chapter Five

My mam picked me up to take me to the hospital the next day. I was perfectly able to drive and get us there myself, but I understood my mam's need to support me in whichever way she could and just do, 'something' when she felt so obviously powerless. Like I said before, sometimes we just need to accept it when others offer help because it helps them too. It's a mustard seed; a tiny gift.

We got to the waiting room of the Breast Clinic. It was jam packed with terrified women, and their companions. The tension was palpable, despite the surrounding chatter. My mam and I seemed to be the only ones having a laugh with each other. I wasn't worried at all. I was extremely relaxed. My mam was nervous although she was trying to hide it. I felt wounded for her. I didn't want her to be afraid. I wasn't. I wished she could step inside my soul and experience the enlightenment and trust that I felt; so that she could feel how well I was, because sometimes words just are not enough, no matter how hard you try to explain it to someone who is fearful.

So, we chatted on and had giggles, observing the pain of the women's suffering around us. At one point, my mam turned to me and commented upon the upset of a woman who had been called into the clinic and had then come out later, crying as she clutched her little blue basket carrying her hospital gown. Her husband was trying to comfort her as best he could. The husband looked terrified. He was huge, burly bald man, strong and powerful looking, but in the face of his wife's worry and upset, his fear was written all over his face: the devastation of her upset. There is nothing worse when you are in love than seeing your loved one suffer; you would literally do anything to help them, even to bearing that suffering instead of them. My mam was incredibly upset to see this woman so distraught. She had seen me so positive from day one (and bloody stubborn!). She had reflected and knew that some folk would take the news extremely badly; like I had also reflected upon and felt bad for the terrified women I had seen. They may have families, dependents, pre-existing health issues, and so on and so forth. For whatever reason, they were all fearful. We all have reasons to be afraid; how will we cope? How will it affect our family life? What if I am unable to work and earn money? Yes, these things are a concern for all of us. But this could be the case with any form of suffering as I discovered when I broke my finger. I was off work for three months, and nearly lost my house because I don't get sick pay from work. Statutory sick pay barely gets you enough bog roll to wipe your ass on! A cancer diagnosis doesn't have to be the be all and end-all! We either sink, swim or tread water and then when God chucks us a life boat with a mustard seed in it, we can choose to climb aboard, no matter how soaked, and cold we are and no matter how long we have been treading water trying to stay afloat if that's what it took for us.

I sometimes think we enlarge issues in our own heads and make them bigger than they truly are. It's perfectly human. It's a fear related response. This can also work on the opposite in the form of false hope by setting unrealistic goals for ourselves, like me for example signing up for the Great North Run. I realistically cannot do it because of my Fibromyalgia and Hoffa's Disease in my knee. I have always wanted to do it, but realistically cannot. Again this comes down to acceptance, rather than change. When we chase impossible dreams, we will always be disappointed, but when we accept what cannot realistically be or do, we begin to accept and live what we realistically can. This leads to a much more fulfilling and positive life. If we continue to try to achieve what we cannot, then we will always feel like failures. But if we work towards what we can achieve, then we will feel fruitful and useful.

In 2010, I ran the Sport Relief Mile. At the time, I believed it was achievable for me. I ran it! I couldn't walk for three days afterwards! I was frigging ill! Crippled! I can't run for s*** and I know I can't but I tried. I didn't allow it to make me feel like a failure though. But I did realise that pushing myself to do something I physically can't do was entirely pointless. I was bedridden for days, in agony and wasted opportunities to do other things within my reach while my body recovered.

In 2013, I participated in the Race for Life and did it for my dad and aunt, and some poochie pals of mine who had been taken too soon. I took six dogs with me, and ambled with my then girlfriend, enjoying it all. She could have run, being younger and fitter than I, but she walked with me and with the dogs. We just took our time. The dogs were absolutely exhausted at the end of it in their pink diamanté collars! We all slept for hours afterwards. I think we did it in one hour and forty minutes.

In 2017, I participated in the Race for Life again, for what would have been my Aunt Barbara's 50th birthday. Again I did it with my dogs. I had long since learned that trying to run would be a disaster! My family and friends who were running took their positions, and I lingered at the back with the walking party, and my boys, Mason and Xander. I would just take my time like before I told myself. But no! Me, being me went on a total mission to beat my previous time! My boys and I pushed ourselves and I beat my time! As I approached the finish line I decided (unwisely!) to run to the finish! My boys began to run too, faster than me and being on lead it was difficult to keep up with them during the excitement of the crowd roaring with support as we ran (I also had to let go of Xander as I tried to keep my hat on my head as I ran!). My boys thought it was the best thing ever! As we crossed the finishing line, my legs gave way and I fell flat on my face in an embarrassing heap! I shouldn't have pushed myself, but I did! I dragged myself out of the way of the other racers as I was told my time of fifty-two minutes. I was over the moon! I was lying flat on my back with my hat over my face in a total heap of sweat and agony! My dogs had gone into a total panic of licking and trying to give me the poochie version of CPR because their pack leader was on the deck! I'm always in a physically and mentally elevated position over them, so when I am on the floor, they automatically presume I am in danger of some sort and try to rescue me. They are so very respectful like that. My dogs would do anything for me!

Seven months later I was to get an injury that meant I would never be able to do it again. Almost a year later I can still barely walk and have to take regular breaks and elevate my leg to keep the swelling down. Although I may now not be able to walk it, let alone run, I can still participate, even if in a wheel chair. There are still options. We must not feel defeated and deny ourselves from embarrassment or prejudices about ourselves or others. Our fight is our own. We cannot compare it to the experience of others. Even if we are fighting the same issues, it does not mean we have to or need to fight in the same way. We all have different tools in our DIY belts. We can help each other to improve our tool belts, but it is up to each of us to learn how to use those tools to our best advantage (little mustard seeds).

As we sat in the clinic waiting room, my mam, and I prayed for these women, especially the distraught woman. I hoped she had an adequate tool belt and that so did her husband to support her. As an empath, to feel others' pain is overwhelming. I had to draw on every strength to stay level in my own soul. As each woman was called in, their dejected faces wounded me. Not one smile or hint of positivity; any attempt at that was just that…an attempt.

Then I was eventually called forward to see my 'titty team'. I was totally relaxed and completely prepared to roll with the punches. The young nurse called us and apologised for our wait. I replied jovially, 'Morning darling, no worries!' and thanked her for holding the door open for us. I had been telling my mam a horse related story as we walked through to the room where my 'titty team' was waiting. I was finishing my story and still finishing it when the team greet us. They seemed surprised to find me so jovial yet again. I introduced my mam to Pauline the fabulous Breast Nurse whom she had not met yet. My consultant began and explained that my CT scan had shown no spread to any internal organs (which I hadn't thought it had!) but that apart from being in my rib bones there were small indications in the back of my neck, but it was totally treatable. I high fived my mam and my consultant. The rest of the team giggled as I continued to crack jokes. My mam was still doing the serious face and voice, which reminded me of Princess Diana somewhat; with the head down pose and upwards look. Obviously, my mam hadn't been there a week earlier to hear the positivity about treatments when I was with my step-daughter Charlotte and I had tried to shut her and her worry up. I had already told her everything and been perfectly honest to my own understanding.

The 'titty team' were then going to discuss with the oncology team about starting my treatment etc and how I might need further tests and scans but then how I might not even need surgery on the offending boob. If it's necessary its end of story! I assured them that I understood everything I had been told. I understand that I come across as quite an unusual individual at times and I get largely misunderstood. I have quite a playful personality and quite happy to take the p*** out of myself. I've had every external insult going so taking the mick out of myself and recognising my own foibles is quite enlightening. People don't always realise how self-aware I actually am. I'm sure there are still things. I have to learn about myself and that is the beauty of the gift of life. Never stop learning, especially about ourselves, because we change and transform. They also don't recognise my academic achievements. I have two university degrees and other qualifications besides. This is not a boast by any stretch, just a statement of fact. Yet, I am judged because I apparently 'don't look like I do or sound like I do'. I am a joggers, boots and hoody type girl on an average day. I don't pretend for anyone. I am just me and will be comfortable in my body and needs. I love my pyjamas and slippers! If I get dressed to go out, I wear a shirt, trousers and dress shoes (and tie if the occasion calls for it). I have short spikey hair and glasses. I mostly wear a cap because I don't like the sun getting in my eyes or dead leaves falling into my hair at work! I am just who I am. Yet, I am judged by many because I don't 'look' like an academic? I'm not saying I am intelligent because I'm not. I'm just saying that I worked hard for the knowledge and understanding I have. I love learning! And every experience I have ever had has been a lesson to me in some ways. *'For those that have eyes to see and ears to hear'*. This is not a statement about the physical by Jesus, but rather an invitation to us to see what we have not seen before and to hear what we have not heard before, in a spiritual sense. It's about recognising the gifts of the mustard seeds that are offered us in whichever way and our ability to see them or hear them. Well over the years I have both seen and heard.

I mean, what does an academically intelligent person looks like, or sound like? Personally I have no idea! Do 'they' expect tweeds? Corduroy pants? Heavy skirts and blouses? Thick ass glasses? Sensible shoes? Boring? A scent of chalk dust? No sense of humour? I just don't know!

What I do know is that I initially felt judged (rightly or wrongly). When Pauline the Breast Nurse, took Charlotte and I into the room to discuss treatments, etc I got the distinct impression that she thought I hadn't understood the conversation with the consultant, especially when I had tried to explain my prohibitive diet etc. I had gone straight to the hospital from work so was dressed as usual in joggers, hoody, boots, cap, and body warmer; in full black outfit. I was my usual scruffy looking mess! Not that I cared!

Pauline explained everything and I totally understood, and I cracked jokes with Charlotte. Pauline looked at me like I was some sort of head case! She asked if I had any questions. I said I did and then I asked her about the Horizons research. We discussed it and I said I wanted to take part and why. I explained that I was a trained Historian, that I had been a teacher, that I had researched and written one book and was researching another one. Her mouth kind of fell open with surprise! I told her I wanted to participate and help the research as I felt it was crucially important. I then told her she had given me the inspiration to begin writing another book to help to support women facing our little fight.

Pauline had looked totally incredulous! When my mam, and I were leaving the clinic upon hearing the good news that the mongrels hadn't gone anywhere horrid, mam starting doing 'the Diana' again; even though I got it all, my mam needed to hear it for her own ears. I told Pauline that I had been in touch with the research team and begun my book in earnest. She genuinely looked blown away! She asked for a signed copy when it was published. I told her she'd be one of the first.

If God wishes my little offering to be published then so be it and I fall on my face before His grace and eternal love. I write only to support and offer mustard seeds where I can. The world can always benefit from more love and understanding and a damn sight less fear!

So, we left the hospital jubilantly and I practically skipped through the waiting room where the frightened women's faces suddenly turned from fear to…I'm not quite sure…surprise? It must be a rare thing to see joy. There's no telling how many times these women had sat there surrounded by fear. I myself had been there on five separate occasions, feeling a wide range of emotions. Who knows what tests they were waiting to have? Or what results they were waiting to hear about? Or what their personal concerns were?

Did they worry about feeling exposed or embarrassed in front of the staff as they bared their breasts for scrutiny? Did they worry that treatments might defeminise them and make them less desirable to their partners? Did they have a fear of needles? All kinds could be racing through their heads' all at once. It's very overwhelming to worry about everything all at once.

When I first saw my GP, I admitted to her that it was hard for me; not to whip my top up, but to admit I knew something was wrong. I had been in the habit of burying my head in the sand. I had done it in two, abusive relationships where I had tried to stay too strong for the wrong reasons. I would not make that mistake again; no matter how hard it was to admit myself and her that I needed help.

I was going to the Breast Clinic a few days after and I had to get my head on straight. It wasn't the end of the world if it wasn't great news. Sure, I was worried. I'm just human like everyone else. But I did a lot of self-reflection and soul-searching in that time. I had to accept that a cancer diagnosis was more than likely and chose to accept that I had to do everything necessary to be healed. God had thrown me a lifeboat filled with mustard seeds. I was damn well getting in it! Treading water was not an option! Neither was sinking! And why try to swim when there is a perfectly capable boat to get into? God would keep me safe. That I just knew. I became unshakeable in my faith. I had always been unshakeable in my faith, but this time was completely different for me. This was my own personal fight and I wanted everyone to hop into the lifeboat with me and share the mustard seeds. I wasn't the only one who needed saving from themselves.

I just knew I'd be alright. Other people may have felt immediate fear and panic, especially my mam and I knew they would. I worried about them and would their faith get them through? They had already seen such loss and devastation (from a variety of sicknesses, not just cancer). I didn't want their fear to overtake their ability to be strong and positive. Fear is a killer, but love is a healer. Love gives us fight; fear gives us defeat. If I wasn't going to be defeated, I didn't want anyone else to be either!

When I'd told my mam about having undergone tests at the hospital (and got a bollocking for going alone) she said angrily, 'If you've got cancer, I'll never speak to God again!' I was mortified!!! I retorted back, 'Don't ever blame God! It's not His fault!' I text her later and begged her again not to blame God. God gets the blame all the time when there is no one left to blame. Now was not the time for a lapse in faith! Especially from the woman to whom I was utterly devoted and who had saved lives before with selfless and nurturing acts. She is self-deprecating and doesn't realise how special she is, although many recognise it in her. My mam is a natural born healer and leader. If I didn't blame God, why should anyone else? S*** happens. We either chose to see things as

104

a curse or a blessing. An opportunity or a failure. I saw my diagnosis as an opportunity; to change me and to help others where I could. *'Lord, make me a channel of your peace':* The Prayer of St. Francis of Assisi.

I was clamming for a coffee, so we went back to my mam's after the hospital, and we started to disperse the positive news to the people who had been waiting to hear. My mam text my brother; he was concerned about how I would cope taking care of my dogs and cats if the chemo made me feel crappy. While my mam was sorting him out, I rang my boss Holly. She was over the moon and started clapping. When I got home to sort my dogs out, I rang Dan at work (which I never do unless necessary) as she knew, I was getting my results. She couldn't hide the initial panic in her voice at first, when she said, 'Hello, is everything alright?' I said, I was ringing with good news. 'Hang on' she said, 'I'm with Gail; I'll put you on speaker!' I knew she met Gail my other friend at work on a Friday, and they would walk together. So, I told them the positive news, and they were jubilant! It's so lovely to be able to share nice things with people. I thanked them both profusely for their love and support.

From day one I hadn't wanted any fuss or fiasco. I never have done if I've ever been poorly or feeling crappy. I hate being faffed over like I'm a helpless child. When I relapsed with my Fibromyalgia, I needed help to do things, and that was fine, but fuss and faff was just annoying. I needed help to heal, not wrapping up in cotton wool. I felt the same now because I was not actually ill. Sore yes, but ill, no. I didn't need to be coddled like I was incapable. Neither did I want anyone to descend into a realm of fear, thinking depressing and negative things. I needed my army of pedigree attack dogs to be fully armed with positivity and strength, ready to stand and fight with me. I was a woman on a mission and with a purpose!

When we have a purpose, we have a reason to fight. When we are without purpose we are already lost. When I was diagnosed with Fibromyalgia, my doctor said, I should medically retire. I laughed and said, 'Then do what? Sit on my useless ass. I think not!' I spoke to my rheumatologist at the hospital, and we sorted out how could I best manage my condition. Then that's what I did! I got my fight back. I had to learn to operate within my limits and at times it's infuriating and frustrating, but not the end of the world.

Neither is my current diagnosis. Yeah! I've got a few mongrels kicking about, but has it held me back or held me down? No, and not bloody likely either! You've got to take the rough with the smooth as they say, but that's just life. We shouldn't feel defeated by the rough. When we walk through stormy waters, all we need to do is watch out for God's life boat and recognise it when arrives. I also have learned that, once we hop aboard that life boat, we are also given an opportunity to help others into it with us as they too weather the storm. The Gospel is a gift to be shared.

I re-examined this philosophy in comparison to the Parable of the Good Samaritan and realised they were the same thing. In the parable, Jesus tells us of a man who was robbed and beaten by bandits as he made a journey. He was left for dead by the roadside. A Levite and a priest travelling the same journey came across him, but did not help him (Levites and priests were affluent men of status). Then a Samaritan man (Samaritans were considered to be foreigners and offensive to the Judeans), stopped by the roadside and

106

took pity on him. He put the man on his humble donkey and took him to the nearest inn, where he asked the innkeeper to take good care of him and bind his wounds to bring him back to health. The Samaritan continued his journey to complete his own task, and then upon his return, he went back to the inn and paid for the treatments and hospitality for the beaten man who had since been healed.

I've seen the parable in a whole new light now. So when God offers us a life boat, we should definitely help others to get in it, especially if they are on a similar journey to ourselves. We can share our mustard seeds with them.

So, let us end this chapter with a final piece of scripture and let us reflect upon it: *'Evil does not grow in the soil, nor does trouble grow out of the ground. No indeed! Man brings trouble on himself, as surely as sparks fly up from a fire'.* Job 5:6-7.

Chapter Six

I was awaiting news from the oncology team as to when I would begin my chemotherapy. I had been advised that I might get a last-minute call if they had a vacancy for me to attend for the treatment. Obviously I would do whatever it took. I had attended the Breast Clinic on the Friday, and they were meeting with the oncology team on the Monday. I had remained positive over the weekend and on a high, but now, I was coming down from that high. That is not to say that I had lost my faith or my positivity at all you understand; merely that I had become a little frustrated! I suppose it's natural to feel that way.

I knew that I might get a call at any moment to attend the hospital for the treatment. I knew my boss and colleagues were incredibly supportive of me, but I must admit that I felt like a burden and inconvenience to them, even though all they wanted was for me to get well. I felt dejected somewhat; not for me, but for them. I was turning their lives upside down too and I didn't want to do that to them at all! In the almost six years I had worked for Holly, I had never taken a day's sick (other than the fiasco of the severed finger!) I had gone to work despite hallucinating with a ridiculous fever due to tonsillitis; food poisoning, a fractured elbow, broken ribs, tummy bugs, costochondritis, sprained ankle, infected ankle, sciatica, trapped nerve in my dodgy shoulder and all the way through Hoffa's disease where I could barely walk or drive without crying or vomiting with pain. I had refused to go to the hospital about my knee until Holly begged me to and berated me for not going already. She had been very supportive during these 'episodes' and appreciated the fact I had come to work and given it my all even when I wasn't well.

But then I'm easily bored! If I were off work from the job I loved, I would just sit around the house moping and wondering how my fur babies were getting on! So I went to work instead and my dogs kept me strong. There's nothing quite like being in the fresh air and in the wilds with a strong pack of highly trained dogs who have always got your back and with wonderful colleagues who make you laugh on daily basis and who also have your back.

I didn't ever want to let them down in anyway. So, I felt dejected waiting to hear news about when my chemo would start. I didn't want it to impact upon them in any negative way when they had lives of their own to live and arrange. They had children and husbands, and partners and issues of their own to be sorting out. I felt awful to be such an inconvenience.

The chemo itself didn't concern me much. I'm not afraid of needles or cannulas or such like, or of sitting for hours on end as it pumped through me: I could read or write, chat on, crack jokes and otherwise occupy myself. I worried about who would take care of my boys if I had to spend the day or overnight in hospital. Xander, my blonde Labrador suffers with extreme separation anxiety. He is Mason's son (he was a happy accident, not a planned breeding…Mason was neutered soon after!) and he was born into my hands on my living room floor, and we have never been parted since. Xander becomes very distressed if he is away from me or his father. When I took him to the vet to be neutered and left him there as I went off to work, he was unimpressed. I warned them about his panic. They said they would sedate him and he would be fine. Hehe! Famous last words! I had dropped him off at 8.30am and then asked when I could ring to check on him. They told me to ring after 12 noon but that he probably wouldn't be ready to collect until after 4 pm due to the sedation and anaesthesia.

Imagine my horror and surprise when the receptionist at the vet's rang me at 11.15 am. I initially panicked asking if Xander was alright and was something wrong? I was assured that the surgery had gone well, and that my boy was perfectly fine and ready for picking up as soon as possible. I thanked her profusely, a little puzzled and told her I would get him as soon as possible because I was still at work.

At 1.45 pm, my phone rang again from the vet. This time, I couldn't hear a word being said! There was a dog in the background absolutely screaming and howling! It was a heart-breaking sound! It was the vet herself ringing me this time. She explained that Xander had become incredibly distressed, and that I needed to collect him as soon as possible! I explained that I was still at work and that I would get him as soon as I could. I could hear him absolutely hysterical in the background. I struggled to hear the vet as she explained how she had needed to take Xander into reception to sit with the receptionist because he was distressing the other animals! I asked her if she could sedate him until I got there. She told me he was already under sedation and still going mental with panic! The vet was truly concerned that he would send himself into cardiac arrest with panic! I got there as soon as I could to collect him, and he was in a state of complete distress! I put Xander in my van with Mason his dad, and he immediately calmed down. I felt bad for the surgery staff experiencing what they did with Xander! He has always been the same! And, so I worry about leaving him; for his own safety and for the sanity of others!

So, receiving chemo made me worry about taking care of my dogs and cats. It was also my brother's concern: his answer was to just to get rid of them all! That's not an answer! My animals are my family. I am never alone when I am with them. They make me happy; they support me, they give me purpose and direction. They are who I get up for in the morning, and who comfort me at night. I do my best to fulfil them and make them happy too by honouring the wild animal in them. I study them and observe them; I learn from them, and they learn from me. I was not going to 'get rid!' I made a commitment to each of the animals in my care that I would never forsake them. I don't ever intend to. God forbid my brother became ill for any reason, I would not demand that he put his young daughter into foster care because I was worried how he'd cope in taking care of her! I view my animals in a similar way to children; except when we devote ourselves to an animal, it is on the understanding that they will always be dependent upon us to fulfil their needs, whereas we rear our children to be separate and independent of us when they are ready.

So the prospect of chemo didn't worry me for myself, it worried me for others. I did not want to be a burden in any way. Even knowing that you have a massive support network to help you out if you needed cannot remove the feeling of being a burden. I had an army of supporters on standby…and I mean an army! But that army had lives and commitments too, as well as their own worries, and concerns.

Maybe I was being too stubborn? Self-reliant when I didn't need to be? Proud? Embarrassed to need support? I'm not sure. What I did know was that I felt guilty. I felt guilty for worrying other people and causing them concern and upset. That may sound ridiculous, as having 'mongrels' is not my choice or God's doing, but for some reason I felt responsible for any wound they may have received because of me.

Upon further self-reflection and self-scrutiny, I realised that this guilt was borne from the deep love and compassion that I felt for my family and friends, especially my mam. I am fiercely protective and devoted to them all. I love them with all my heart and soul. Over the years I had tried to protect and support them as best I could and knew how. Anything at any time! I wasn't quite sure how to feel about not being able to fulfil the role I had created for myself if I was to feel poorly. Maybe that's why I felt guilty and responsible? I don't know really. Maybe I had created an unachievable role for myself and now, I was facing the possibility that I couldn't live up to it? I don't really know. All I know is that I felt guilty of inadvertently hurting those I loved. But maybe I am over-analysing? Maybe it just all boils down to this simple explanation: when we truly love, we feel truly guilty about hurting those we love, whether we mean to or not. If we do not truly love, then we cannot feel guilty over hurting someone. If this is simply the case, does this mean that guilt is a sign of our true humanity and perfectly natural to those who love? I believe this may be the simpler and more reasonable answer. I certainly hadn't set out to hurt anybody, but, yet I felt guilty.

Despite my mongrel diagnosis, I would still do what I could to support those who are needed it. It didn't change me as a person or how I viewed life, or my protective streak. I didn't want to feel dejected, but I suppose that's just normal, being purely human. I couldn't be on a positive high all the time. I had to *accept* there would be times when I would feel physically and emotionally crappy.

Feeling dejected didn't last very long though; these things never really do, but some folk hold on to negativity because they don't have anything positive to cling to instead. I find that a real shame. There is always something positive to cling to if we look hard enough for it.

I discussed earlier how I had struggled to gain weight and how I had then been correct that I in fact had achieved a weight gain. I felt like I was continually gaining. My rings were tighter, my ass and ribs weren't as bony and my mam had given me some fleecy trouser bottoms that would usually have been on the loose side for me. I got up for work on the Monday morning and upon hearing the weather report that it would rain all day, I went to put my wellies on. I couldn't get my feet in at first and then when I did, they were far too small and tight for me and extremely uncomfortable! I was forced to opt for my work boots instead, no matter how damp my feet got. My other two pairs of wellies randomly leak. Then I tried to get my work boots on and had to loosen the shoe laces for the second time in a week because they had become too tight as well, although the boot still actually fit me.

I got weighed again and discovered that I had gained three pounds in four days! That made ten pounds over the previous three weeks! I couldn't believe I had gained almost a stone in such a short space of time when I had struggled for years to gain weight! I felt great! I swore to keep up the good work! I was jubilant! I was not going to waste the opportunities that had been given me to improve myself physically, mentally, emotionally or spiritually. I just needed new wellies!

This may not seem like much to some, but when you have struggled with your weight and don't feel your best, it's a huge issue. I'd spent most of my life around people bitching on that they were too fat. As a woman, this is pretty hard to escape from! I had it at school from unhappy teenagers (both male and female) who were desperate to lose weight and change their physiques and there was constant chatter about 'calories'. It was bloody irritating! Then when I entered my working adult life, I couldn't bear to sit and eat with the other women because they bitched on incessantly about weight clubs, calories, exercise classes and such. They had *no* other conversation in them! They judged what I ate because I was thinner than they.

My first partner constantly bitched on about her weight and about how unhappy she was at being heavier than she wanted to be but still drank copious amounts of fattening cider and cheap ass wine and sat on her drunken ass all day, eating crap in the meantime. She joined the gym and was still unhappy. I got sick and tired of listening to her whingeing on about her weight constantly! It wasn't a rare topic; it dominated virtually every communication we had, and I felt like I was going around in circles in my head as she sought constant reassurance; pointless reassurance from me because no matter what I said, she was still going to be unhappy in her own soul.

My ex-wife was exactly the same! Yes, my wife was heavier than I but it didn't bother me…it only bothered her. But my wife was also a secret eater and would hide massive popcorn packets and crisp packets beneath the sofas and then pretend she hadn't 'treated herself'. She hated that I was thinner than her, despite my massive appetite. She bitched on constantly about her weight, and it got on my nerves. She was in control of her own intake and constantly accused me of trying to make her feel fat; like if I didn't want a dessert after our meal, and she did, or if we were out shopping and, she wanted doughnuts and I didn't. It was bloody infuriating!

After my dad passed over, I put on two and a half stone. My kickboxing twice a week had stopped because my instructor had sold the club and I had sustained a painful back injury. I started to feel sluggish and achy. I knew I needed to lose the weight to control my Fibromyalgia. My then wife's solution was for me to attend Slimming World with her. Erm…no thanks! I had been to meetings before in a purely observatory capacity or to wait for my wife. It was annoying to listen to the same few people bitch on about how they hadn't lost weight…but then hear that they had gone to fast food places, or ordered takeaway, or just fancied a bit of cake every day, or gone out for a meal and then wondered why they had put on weight! But they were otherwise sticking to the plan! It bloody p***ed me off! My wife was one such person! I got it in both ears day in and day out! My sister-in-law spent on average one hundred pound a month on her weight loss plan for six years, and ended up four stone heavier! What on Earth is the bloody point?

I refused point-blank to attend meetings! I told my wife, I refused to sit in a room full of bitching 'fat' women who wondered why they were still 'fat' when they didn't follow the plan properly. They were there to achieve something for themselves and paying to do so, but they were using it as a social club to bitch on about themselves. I actually wanted to achieve something and I didn't need them to do it! You can only, have so much patience when you have heard the words 'I'm so fat!' from virtually every woman you've ever known for years on end. It was like a stuck irritating record in my head!

So, I refused to attend meetings. I scrutinised the plan that I had become so used to discussing with my wife and utilised it. I lost two and a half stone in eight weeks. My wife was furious, as she had not lost similarly in the same time frame. But she had been lying to herself and secret snaffling on the sly. She also thought that if she went to the gym, it gave her licence to eat as much crap as she wanted. It doesn't work like that!

Don't get me wrong, I have absolutely nothing against 'overweight' folk! What is an issue for me is folk bitching on about things that are well within their reach, if they really want to achieve them! It's like constantly listening to someone bitch on about having a constant headache because they keep beating themselves over the head with a hammer! Just put the f***ing hammer down!!! I'm not being uncompassionate at all! Some people really do have a hard time achieving their goals; but when people are given the opportunity and choose to sit there bitching instead, it p***es me off! I have heard it my entire life how people are unhappy with their weight or physique. They know what to do to change it and yet don't do it! They give constant excuses; I've been on my holidays, I'm upset, I'm happy and celebrating something: any excuse! What exactly do they want from the people they are bitching to? A don't worry about it, you are lovely as you are? Yes, you need to lose a few pounds? Neither is a suitable answer: if you compliment them, they still bitch that their pants don't fit! But if you agree with them, they get all offended! So what do they hope to achieve by bitching on about themselves? I honestly have no idea!

I was on the opposite scale of trying to gain weight. Although various people would tell me I was too thin for my height, I actively tried to gain and ask advice where ever I could; but no one is interested in helping you gain when they are all trying to lose! There was limited advice out there for weight gain, especially for a prohibitive diet. It p***ed me off when people would say, 'Eeh, I wish I weighed that!' Really people, no you wouldn't! I looked bloody awful and felt bloody awful; physically and emotionally!

I wanted to get fight ready and gain weight to deal with the chemo and so far I had been gaining now that I understood what had caused the loss in the first place. I prepared myself to see the oncologist with humour in my heart.

My mother's partner had telephoned her and asked if I had heard from or seen the 'ornithologist'. My mam had burst out laughing, much to his chagrin. She laughed 'The ornithologist? Why would she be seeing an ornithologist? You do know what an ornithologist is don't you?' He replied that they were cancer specialists. My mam laughed and replied, 'No darling, you mean oncologist; an ornithologist is a bird expert and bird watcher!' He was very embarrassed! But he took it light heartedly, laughing, 'Well she does like birds (of the female variety); besides, both words begin with an 'o' and end in a 'gist'!' So from now on, I'm not seeing the oncologist, but the ornithologist! I laughed my little socks off!

I then got a telephone call confirming my date to see the 'ornithologist', which was to discuss treatment and consent. This kind of ended my previous frustration and dejection. A few hours later, I got a call from the MRI department. The 'ornithologist' wanted me to have a further scan. It was arranged for three weeks hence. I wasn't told what it was for or why. My anxiety peaked yet again, despite my joviality and acceptance of the fact.

The next day, Pauline the Breast Nurse telephoned me to inform me of the new MRI (of which I already knew about). She informed me that it would be on my liver. Then when I got my letter, it also indicated my spine and lumbar too. I became afraid, my anxiety spinning out of control. I began to think all kinds of things, which is not helpful! But none of the reasons for this had been explained to me, so I was just playing a guessing game with myself. I knew the mongrels had not spread anywhere nasty so they weren't looking for mongrels on the scan. So what were they looking for?

I had my own wonderings. When I had seen the 'titty team' for my CT results, they said that the CT had shown up something concerning my hips, femurs and liver and a few, 'mongrels' in my vertebrae. Obviously I was honest with them about my fondness for a few beers after work because you can't be fibbing about that sort of stuff, so obviously my liver function was going to be a concern, especially given that I was on five medications for my Fibromyalgia symptoms. So that bit I understood! But I did not understand the rest; although upon researching (as I do!), I realised that this might be because I was prone to osteoarthritis or osteoporosis and may already be showing signs of it in the areas, they wanted to MRI.

This is very important to treatment, especially as I was post-menopausal and a good candidate for brittle bones, and that I also had a family history of osteoarthritis. In the meantime I felt great in myself if a little sore in more places than usual. My head, however, was a different matter! Although I remained positive, I began to find everything a bit overwhelming in a psychological sense. I hated being faffed with and fussed over at the best of times! I was beginning to feel like a lab rat trapped in a cage; rightly or wrongly so. I started to feel more dejected than I would like to feel.

It's hard not to panic and feel anxious at times. I felt like I was being pushed from pillar to post on a daily basis with either telephone calls or appointments. It was all becoming a bit overwhelming. This is where you need your army to keep you afloat with positivity and reassurance. Dan was an excellent support with this, reassuring me that the extra tests, etc were just to cover all bases and make sure they were taking care of everything single little thing that could be affected by or related to the mongrels. I suppose they needed to be sure of things for their research too…as what helps me could help another person in a similar situation.

It was this re-thinking that helped me stay focused and positive. I was undergoing all of this because it may help someone else in the future. My body and soul had and would always belong to God, so if this was part of the Lord's Will; His Will be done.

Chapter Seven

I had pondered the saying 'Every cloud has a silver lining' as I further ruminated upon my situation. I realised that I had not understood it in its broadest context and applicability. I had merely seen it in a physiological and meteorological context. Yeah, clouds reflect light, right? But what does this actually mean?

Well, let me explain my understanding, as I now saw it. Clouds are seen as a negative thing (especially in rainy Britain!) It brings rain and cooler temperatures, and we moan on about it when we get cold and wet. But in the summer, when there are hosepipe bans because it hasn't rained in forever, we miss those pesky clouds, praying for water and a cooler night's sleep, or day's work! We have the blessing of indoor plumbing and water literally on tap. But then we have equatorial countries who pray for clouds because it hasn't rained in decades, and they have no water at all.

So clouds are a life-giving necessity. We must see the arrival of clouds as a gift from God, because that cloud is about to pour out God's blessings upon us: life sustaining water which feeds the crops and animals that feed us, cool us down, and fulfils a multitude of other needs, whether we know we need it or not.

Like I've said, having mongrels gave me an opportunity to re-evaluate my life and my failings and missed opportunities. It gave me an opportunity to change what I could and use that new-found experience to help others who are in a cloudy place and merely seeing only the dark that a cloud can cast without seeing the blessings behind it.

I had to approach my oncology appointment seeing the sunshine breaking through the clouds. The previous week had been filled with anxiety, with chopping and changing, new tests and new scans arranged etc. It made me paranoid! So when I attended my oncology appointment, I felt no less eased but entered it with humour as always.

My mother and I met with the doctor and two of the Breast Nurses. He explained about the mongrels after asking me some pertinent questions about lifestyle, etc. He told us that the mongrels couldn't be entirely cured but the treatment was to control it. My mam and I both said, 'OH!' He asked if that hadn't already been explained in the Breast Clinic by the consultant. We both said in unison 'Erm no!' He then went on to explain that because the mongrels had settled in the bones in a few places, it was harder to shift. Despite the fact that the consultant in the Breast Clinic had told us that the CT scan hadn't shown any signs of mongrels going anywhere else (although something had shown in my hips and femur but did not look like mongrels) the oncologist had ordered the next MRI obviously to check for further bone mongrels in my hips, spine and liver and pretty much said, so without really saying it. He was also under the impression that I hadn't been suffering from any pain in my hips or lower back for some reason, although I had informed the consultant at the Breast Clinic that since the severe injury to my knee, my walking had

121

changed completely and resulted, in pain in my hips and lower back (from which I had already suffered for years due being flat-footed and having one leg already longer than the other. My knee injury had further shortened my shorter leg; so as well as being a wonky walker, I was a wonky worker! Most of my jobs had been very manual over the previous twenty years and osteoarthritis ran in my family. My GP refused to test me for it. My mam agreed that my pain levels had massively increased in my hips and lower back as a result of my knee injury.

The doctor was very reassuring and positive about treatment, but as my own particular mongrels had shown some peculiar anomalies in the biopsies, that they couldn't explain, he would need to discuss with his colleagues what treatment plan would be the most suitable. He ordered that I also have an ECG prior to beginning chemo. And yet another round of bloods was taken!

I left the hospital with my mam feeling more confused than anything else. My mam was stuck on 'incurable'. He hadn't said incurable, he had said, 'not entirely curable'. In my world, they were two very different things! I was confused because I had been told two different understandings of my CT scan. What on Earth was I supposed to think? One version was more positive than the other.

I decided to continue following the positive. I was not going to be defeated by any stretch!!! Not entirely curable my arse!!! The mongrels were going to be crushed by the Hand of God whether they liked it or not. There was no two ways about it in my soul. I spoke to my friend Clare about this new development as I was so confused, by the two different interpretations. She proffered that maybe the oncologist was hedging his bets onto the worst possible case scenario and would rather tell me the severity of the situation than provide me with false hope by not telling me that it could have escalated, hence the need for another MRI to get a clearer picture. Clare proffered that it's much nicer to tell someone good news than bad, so if they start with the negative and it's as negative, as expected, then at least the patient is already informed, but if it's positive, then so much better for both patient and doctor!

It made perfect sense to me! It was entirely logical! I could not be convinced that the mongrels had wandered themselves off further, in pretty much the same way that my sodium levels would not convince me of a wandering off to my kidneys. My hips and back had been hurting because of my incredibly bad posture too! I had sat for nine months in the same position with my leg elevated and my back hunched, putting unnecessary pressure on my hips and lumbar region. Once I readjusted my position, sitting up straighter and with my knee appropriately elevated to a comfortable height, the pains I had been experiencing minimised in just two days. I still experienced some muscle twinges as my body readjusted from the torture I had inflicted upon it, but again this is also a normal part of having Fibromyalgia and experiencing widespread pain for no apparent reason! The pains I had experienced were worse than any mongrel related pain, which I merely experienced as a slight tenderness in the affected areas. I knew the difference: hence I could not be convinced that there was mongrelisation anywhere else.

My attitude may sound arrogant and pompous to some and for that I apologise, but over the years I had spent a lot of time in self-reflection and self-scrutiny. I had come to know my body, mind and soul a lot better than I had. When you have a long-term chronic illness, you learn to become very aware of slight changes, twinges, aches or pains. You also learn how to adapt to the limitations of your body. You have pay intense attention to yourself in a way that people without a chronic illness do not have to. Everyone experiences suffering in their own unique way and one thing I have learned is never to assume that anyone's pain is lesser or greater than your own. Pain is an equalising experience. Pain is pain, no matter how we experience it, whether it be physical, mental, emotional or spiritual.

I felt deeply wounded for those who were in pain, especially those in a similar situation to myself. I prayed for them and hoped they could find positivity and strength. There were a lot of people who were terribly afraid upon awaiting test results, getting sent for more tests, getting told why they needed more tests and then the terror of 'the wait' each time. It's incredibly stressful and indeed worrying. Being human, we cannot just over-ride the 'fight or flight' instinct in our physiology. We again have to choose our response. Do we stand and fight? Or do we flee? If we choose to stand and fight, we may still be afraid. But that's ok. It's normal. At least we are still standing up for ourselves as best we can. We can flee, but we are still afraid. The threat is still there, lurking around the corner, pursuing us, feeding upon our fear and negativity: so the further we try to flee. We may even destroy our own selves before the threat does because we have driven ourselves insane trying to run from the inescapable. The reality is that the only thing, we can never truly run from is ourselves. If we stand and fight despite our fear, we are honouring our own humanity and helping others to fight too.

We can be examples of positivity to each other and therein lies our biggest weapon: love. Those who flee cannot love because the fear overtakes them and consumes them. They cannot build an army of support as they push everyone away looking for a way out. But those who fight build an army of love, and as the saying goes 'Love conquers all things'.

I had chosen to stand and fight. There was no point trying to flee; the mongrels were still going to be fighting their little fight. I had to fight back by whatever means, even if that meant being worried or afraid at times. I was waiting to have my ECG appointment on the Tuesday following my appointment with the oncologist. Then after my ECG, I was to see the oncologist in the afternoon to discuss my treatment plan.

As I was driving to the hospital for my ECG, I popped a music CD into the player. It was a compilation, I had mixed myself. The second song was, *'Rise'* by Katy Perry. I had always loved the song and viewed it as powerful and prayerful. As I drove, the song took on a new meaning for me. It described how I felt about my current fight. I would like to share those lyrics with you **(all credit and copyright to Katy Perry, her producers and company etc):**

"I won't just survive! Oh, you will see me thrive! Can't write my story I'm beyond the archetype. I won't just conform! No matter how you shake my core 'Cause my roots, they run deep, oh!

Oh, ye of so little faith, Don' doubt it, don't doubt it! Victory is in my veins I know it, I know it. And I will not negotiate I'll fight it, I'll fight it I will transform!

When, when the fire's at my feet again And the vultures all start circling, They're whispering, you're out of time. But still, I rise. This is no mistake, no accident. When you think the final nail is in, think again. Don't be surprised, I will still rise!

I must stay conscious! Through the madness and chaos. So I call on my angels, They say

Oh, ye of so little faith Don't doubt it, don't doubt it! Victory is in your veins You..."

I found the lyrics to be quite relevant to how I felt: *'I won't just survive, you will see me thrive'*. I felt very much this way. Mongrels had transformed me into taking better care of myself. I was gaining weight and positivity; people were regularly commenting on how well I looked and on the sparkle that was back in my eyes. *'Victory is in my veins, I know it'*: the fight begins from within and *'I'll fight it, I'll fight it'*. It's a song about staying strong and not doubting what you already know in your own soul, even if sometimes it's hard to maintain that faith, primarily in yourself and what you already know in your soul to be true.

The ECG itself was quick and painless. It was another 'boobs out' job with the ultrasound gel on, but otherwise quite harmless. The physiologist wasn't chatty in the slightest and kept sighing as if thoroughly bored by the whole proceeding. She was kind and professional of course, but not particularly talkative at all. She must do at least one hundred ECG's a day over her shift, so I can imagine that trying to maintain hundreds of different conversations on a daily basis must become quite a chore if you aren't particularly chatty to start with. She smiled politely at my few little jokes and waffling on, but then I became quiet and just allowed her to do her job quietly. She advised me that I would be receiving further ECGs as my treatment progressed. That was fine!

Interestingly though, she said it all depended on the doctor who was treating me and what they wanted. I pondered that for a little while in light of a conversation I had participated in with a client whom I am incredibly fond of, the day before I had my ECG.

She had described her experience with doctors while her husband had been treated for terminal lung cancer. She had an opinion that doctors would treat you according to their own personal agendas, and what they wanted to achieve by way of a cure. Her basic implication was that sufferers are merely 'guinea pigs' to test their research, medications, and theories upon in the struggle to be the best and, most recognised in the business. So her chat with me had made me think a little.

When I saw the oncology doctor, he was truly lovely. He described my treatment plan in detail. He told me that my red and white cell counts were a tiny bit low and that I may need transfusions or iron tablets if it was to become an issue. He went on to describe the side effects of the chemotherapy and the dangers of infections. I would most likely lose my hair, I might feel sickly, experience flu-like symptoms, tiredness, lethargy, aches and pains and so forth. I laughed and said, 'Pretty much like having Fibromyalgia then...but with the hair loss!' He laughed and agreed. I wasn't fazed by any of it.

I was worried about work and the risk of infection, despite the fact that my dogs are very well-behaved and my van is kept immaculate. There was always the risk of being inadvertently scratched or caught on something. We have multiple First Aid kits to care of ourselves and the dogs, but what if this was not enough to protect me from an incredibly reduced immune system? Accidents invariably happen, even if they are just sometimes minimal little cuts or scratches from trees, branches or bushes. Anyway, I was upping the ante on van cleanliness and taking every precaution possible with myself.

My family and friends were a fantastic help in getting my house, 'chemo ready'. They wanted to ensure that everything I came into contact with inside and outside my home was not going to harm me in any way, so Operation Bleach Party began in earnest. I must admit that, I found it is an entirely strange and disconcerting feeling to have people in my home cleaning it from top to bottom. At times, it was very frustrating and stressful as they moved things from places, threw stuff out and generally operated around me. It was difficult to relinquish my own home into the hands of others. I've always felt very intimately attached to my home and I've never liked anyone faffing about in it (my own ex-wife wasn't allowed to clean or hoover...generally because she made more mess in the process than she actually tidied!) So, I was a tad precious at times. All they wanted to do was help, but nevertheless, it is not easy to hand over control when the only thing you really can control is what goes on inside your own home when your body is rebelling against you. I felt a bit lost and helpless during this process as I couldn't control their need to just *do* something.

In the meantime, I waited for a chemo start date. I was invited to the hospital on the Friday I was due my next MRI for a blood transfusion because I was anaemic. It had been a very stressful and overwhelming week getting, 'chemo ready' and all I wanted to do was rest, have some space and to do some spiritual reflection.

Chapter Eight

On the Friday morning my mother accompanied me to the Chemotherapy Day Unit to comfort and support me during the blood transfusion and then later on, the MRI scan. We were welcomed into the unit by a lovely nurse who showed us around the toilets, kitchen and treatment room. It was 9.30am and very quiet with only one other lady awaiting treatment at that time. She also greeted us cheerfully and we reciprocated her greeting.

The treatment room was painted a pastel green with plush green reclining armchairs. The only things that made it look like a hospital room were the IV stands placed by the armchairs, the privacy curtains, the hygiene sink and the hospital computer. Trolleys and files were escorted about as necessary, but otherwise the room was very elegant, relaxing and comfortable. The few chairs and tables were placed around the edges of the room allowing the staff to view the patients at all times and ensure easy access amongst them with no obstructions.

The nurse made me comfortable in my chair with a pillow behind my back and one to rest my right arm on (the cannula was to be placed in the back of my non-dominant hand). The nurse chatted to me about what they had to do etc. and we all talked generally and casually amongst ourselves as the nurse placed the cannula and told me she needed to take a blood sample to get my blood type and then cross match it appropriately before they could order my blood. I was told this might take some time. That was fine! The nurse was also aware that I had an MRI scan due at 4.30 pm, so, they hoped to get my blood sooner rather than later as the transfusions of two units needed to go in over several hours.

As the nurse chatted on to us about what needed to be done, we were approached by a tall, older, blonde lady who inserted herself into the conversation, introduced herself and told me she was the counsellor and art therapist. She said with a beaming smile 'How's the patient?' I laughed as I replied, 'I'm not a patient, I'm a stubborn fighter!' She smiled broadly again as she responded, 'I can see where your head is at!' She would come and have 'a little chat' with me later once the nurse was finished sorting me out. She did come back a little later to ask if I would like to get involved with some art therapy which consisted of making a stamp from clay, etching it with a design, rolling it in ink and then applying it to paper in order to make a little box. I said, I would give it a go! So she arrived back with a tray full of clay, tools, inks and the paper. So, I proceeded to play with clay, tools and ink! Great fun!

It was going to be a while before my blood arrived, so we were invited to make a brew and help ourselves to the selection of munchies in the well-stocked kitchen. So my mam went off to make us a coffee and when she came back, we just chatted on, laughed, giggled, and told each other stories, shared memories and anecdotes and generally had a bit of fun as the unit filled up with other patients and the

130

nurses flitted around us in a steady, professional manner, but always with good cheer and humour and constantly checking in with all of us, even when they didn't need to be directly involved with our care. You'd hear them engaging with patients as they walked by doing something else, even if was just a quick 'You alright there Rachel?' or 'You okay there John?' and so on and so forth.

Some folk had family or friends with them and some people went in unaccompanied. Whatever they needed for their own comfort and peace of mind. Some folk receiving treatment may not have any family to comfort and support them at any time during the process and so, it was essential that the environment they were entering was friendly, welcoming and supportive. Some folk may have comfort and support outside the treatment room, but for one reason or another, were unable to have someone accompany them.

Several brews and conversations with my mam later, at 1.00 pm, a tall, handsome, young gentleman strode into the middle of the busy room where the nurses had their backs to the door tending to their patients and shouted 'Listen up everyone, the blood is here!' My nurse shouted back, 'It's for Rachel!' and the young man was quickly relieved of his delivery by the nearest nurse. My nurse came over quickly to take my observations before the blood was administered: heart rate, blood pressure and temperature. This had to be done before the blood went in, then again fifteen minutes after the beginning of the administration and then again at the end of the unit of blood. I needed two units so this procedure would take place twice. The blood also needed to be checked against my hospital bracelet and then double-checked by two nurses (to make sure the correct person received the correct blood).

There are several blood types so the recipient has to be matched carefully to the donor blood. I have a rare blood type which they call, 'Universal blood' whereby any other recipient can receive my blood type in an emergency and be ok, but my blood type can only receive my blood type and nothing else. It's a bit like having three different types of car: a diesel will only run on diesel, a petrol car can run on leaded or unleaded and if you try to put any sort of fuel into an electric car, you'll probably blow it up, let alone disable the engine! So say I'm like an old classic petrol car that is only equipped to handle leaded petrol; I can only have leaded petrol. However, you might be a new model Audi with a catalytic converter. You generally use unleaded, but in an emergency, you can use leaded petrol because of the converter, without it harming you. (I have NO idea about cars but that's about as close an analogy that makes sense to me).

As the blood had arrived late, this would inevitably have a knock-on effect as to the timing of my MRI scan. I was going to be late for it! Once it was administered, I was observed further for any adverse reactions. Even when you receive your own blood type, there is a tiny chance that your body might not be very chuffed with it because it isn't blood of your very own and might reject it very quickly. My own blood was quite happy to welcome new blood to the party, however and even happier when the lunch trolley came around!

I was a tad munchy by this point, and my mam had also gone to the shop to get me some crisps and chocolate. I proceeded to stuff my face. As I was eating my lunch, the counsellor came back to demonstrate how to make the box now that I had created my little stamped pages. I found her intrusion to be quite inappropriate as I was eating my lunch, but she seemed to have no regard for the etiquette of leaving folk to eat in peace! She was determined to get my little box made, but the ink wasn't dry yet, so she left me with the template of the one she had demonstrated. Finally, she left us to finish my lunch!

My mam and I continued to chat and laugh with each other and my mam started to create the folds for the box that is, until she got covered in wet ink! The project came to a halt to be attempted later on. Then the counsellor came back about an hour later and again inserted herself into the conversation without invitation but with her usual beaming smile saying to me 'So how are you coping with your diagnosis?' I replied that I was absolutely fine. She commented upon my Rosary Beads and enquired into my faith, also asking questions of my mother who had told her that I was incredibly intelligent and philosophical with a deep faith. The counsellor quickly realised that I did not need counselling and departed!

The blood transfusion was definitely going to make me late to my scan and so the staff rang down to the MRI department to inform them of the fact. My nurse also still needed to talk to me about treatment and what to expect. She seemed to have little check box list of things that she was obliged by law to discuss with me and give me the opportunity to ask questions if I needed to. She discussed with me what treatments I would be receiving, and why they performed them over two days on the first cycle (this was to check and monitor any adverse reactions, so they would know which treatments had caused it); I was advised that I would definitely lose my hair and a cold cap was offered (losing my hair was not a concern for me, but it might be for others). A cold cap could be worn during the treatment to minimise the drug reaching the hair follicles and slow down hair loss, but it did not guarantee no hair loss at all. The treatment would make me infertile (I already was, so it was a non-issue) and so, I was asked how I felt about that. Obviously there are ways for a patient to preserve their fertility outside their body, and this could be offered to individuals who required that support, but I did not need that. The treatment would significantly reduce my immune system and so make me more prone to infection. It would not make me neutropenic (that is to say, destroy my immune system in its entirety and leave me extremely vulnerable). I was given a Chemo Card to carry at all times in the event, I felt unwell or was concerned for any reason. The nurse asked if my mam would like a card too: in unison we both replied, 'Yes!' I knew my mam would need one for her own peace of mind. I was given a wig voucher (not that I was bothered about wearing a wig). I have a lovely selection of random hats and bandanas! I was also advised to purchase a digital thermometer to keep an eye on my temperature as chemotherapy can mask the symptoms of infection, but temperature cannot lie!

The nurse knew she was preaching to the converted, as I was able to understand and articulate the reasoning behind why they did things the way they did and discuss it all rationally and with clarity. She found it quite refreshing and explained that some patients had no understanding at all of their diagnosis how to take their medication or how to protect themselves. One such individual was the gentleman sitting in the chair to my left. He was a nice enough man, but unable to assist at all in his own treatment and lacked the capacity to understand what he was being told and therefore participate in a rational conversation about it. His personal hygiene left a lot to be desired: he was an older gentleman in his late fifties, wearing brown unwashed trousers, dirty training shoes that had once been white and a faded yellow, unwashed T-shirt. He wore black worn braces with his trousers. He was balding with a ring of scruffy unwashed and unbrushed hair circling the back of his head from his ears. He had a greyish yellow beard and moustache and when he smiled, his teeth looked like carved stumps of uneven mahogany in his mouth and his tongue was stained dark brown too. His fingers were all stained dark brown and his fingernails were black with dirt. The exterior of his elbows was thick of dirt in the creases of his skin and beyond. The nurse found him to be hard work as she was trying to explain what was going on to him. As he was only in the next seat to me, you could hear her repeatedly asking him if he could first hear her and secondly if he understood what she was telling him. He just stared blankly or gave a brief, 'Yeah'. He obviously had no idea and neither did the young lady accompanying him (I presumed her to be his daughter as she was equally as unwashed and unkempt, although a lovely sociable girl). He just didn't seem to understand (or care?) that good personal hygiene was necessary to ensure his long-term health and well-being.

I'm certainly not judging this gentleman's lifestyle choices, merely pointing out that some people are unable to participate for whatever reason in their own treatment. They seemed unwilling or unable to fight for themselves. He was a nice enough man though and engaged me in conversation quite readily about food, commenting that whenever he happened to look in my direction, I was always eating. Me and my mam had a good laugh with him about this. I certainly wouldn't reject a conversation with him just because he hadn't been washed. He knew what his circumstances were? Maybe homeless? There had to be a reason for his state of extreme disarray, and I was unwilling to judge him based solely on outward appearances.

On the other side of the room were two other older gentlemen. One was tall, handsome, well-dressed and well-groomed with an air of solid dignity and the other was a shorter more rotund gentleman with a small grey moustache. He was casually dressed in jeans, T-shirt and a baseball cap and spoke to the other man as if they had known each other for some time. I could see them staring over at me occasionally; sometimes disapproving, sometimes trying to work out if I was male or female! Short spikey haired, casually dressed lesbians wearing a shirt and jeans were not a species of human they had come across before. They looked at me with perpetual confusion and disdain. I had gotten used to these looks over the years! I felt judged, but I got the impression that they didn't actually realise they were actively doing it as they discussed me (they plainly didn't realise I could actually hear them doing this either from across the other side of the room! I can also lip-read reasonably well, growing up with two deaf aunts) I smiled politely at them. They didn't know what to make of me or how to respond to me, despite my greetings as they had arrived onto the unit earlier.

Finally, the blood was finished and I said my goodbyes to the staff and patients in order to attend for my scan. As I walked out of the unit, I heard the shorter rotund man say to the other man 'I told you it was a girl!' I was an 'it' all of a sudden. I stifled a laugh as I walked out of the room with my mam and headed to the MRI department.

As per usual I was asked to strip to my underwear and put on a back-fastening gown. It was typically cold in the department. I knew this scan was a 'head first' job, which I did not like at all! I was laid on the bed in a neck rest and with a knee support to keep my spine and hips as flat to the bed as possible. The whole scan would take about an hour, I was told. They were to do my spine and lumber first, then the liver. So off I went into the scanner where I was blasted with draughty cold air, surrounded by loud noises (even though I had headphones on and the radio) and weird vibrations of the machine and bed. After forty minutes I was withdrawn and informed that they would now scan my liver, which would take another twenty minutes. The radiographer placed something the size of a remote control over my liver and then went to retrieve a bigger device. It was colossal and heavy as she placed it over my upper body. The only thing, I could compare to was the under-shell of a Teenage Mutant Ninja Turtle! I laughed and said, 'So which ninja turtle do you want to be today? I'm going to be Raphael! I'm liking the red cos I've just had blood!' She had no idea where to put her face and just laughed. The younger male radiographer chimed in cheerfully, 'I'll be Donatello; red is usually my favourite colour, but I can be purple just for today!' I stifled a giggle as I was slid back into the scanner where you have to stay exceptionally still (which is very difficult for a Fibromyalgia sufferer who suffers from involuntary spasms!) I was asked to breathe in and out and hold my breath on the exhale multiple times during the scan. My ribs ached from the pressure of unnatural breathing and the weight of the 'shell' on my chest. I was reminded somewhat of Blessed Margaret Clitherowe, a martyr from York who refused to renounce her Catholic faith in the reign of Queen Elizabeth I. She was executed publicly by being crushed to death beneath a heavy door weighted with boulders. A cruel and horrid death. Her house still stands in The Shambles and I have gone there to pray when I have visited York.

Finally, it was completed and I was allowed to go and get dressed and have my cannula taken out. It had been a very long day for me and my mam and we didn't get home until after 7.00 pm. I just wanted to relax and put my feet up. I felt great in myself, but tired from such a long day. I couldn't shake the image of Blessed Margaret Clitherowe from my mind and how I felt in the scanner for some reason. I was reminded of sacrifice. We can either sacrifice ourselves or sacrifice someone else. We can either sacrifice *for* ourselves or sacrifice *for* someone else, whether we choose to sacrifice ourselves or someone else for whatever reason.

Several Biblical characters sprang to mind as I pondered this. The first one was Abraham; the Father of Faith. He was asked by God to sacrifice his only son Isaac to prove his faith and trust. He was dismayed at having been asked to do this, but he offered his only son on an altar and had raised the knife to slay him when God stopped him. God knew that he would have done it: the first proof that it's the thought that counts! Abraham acted for himself in order to prove his loyalty. This particular story also is the fore-runner to God sacrificing His own only Son, an act He does follow through with, making Jesus the ultimate sacrifice. This time, Jesus was sacrificed for the sake of humanity and their redemption. When we sacrifice, it is because something greater must be achieved by it, even if we don't understand the why's and wherefores of that sacrifice.

A true sacrifice is made with love, even if we don't always want to do it and it scares us. It is not a compromise where agreement is reached between parties to keep both sides appeased. A sacrifice is an offering, a gift, from one party to another. The sacrifice must be truly precious to the one who offers it or it is a meaningless gift: like the rock star who gives £10,000 of his £80,000,000 fortune to a children's Ward. Not much of a sacrifice, when you think about it! He's not exactly going to miss the money. Yet, he is celebrated for having done so! A truer sacrifice is the impoverished single father who doesn't eat for three days because he would rather his young daughter have a hot meal when she comes home from school. Or the firewoman who runs back into a burning building at the risk of her own life in order to save a trapped child. Or the brother who offers his kidney to his ill sister because she would die without it. These are true sacrifices; people offering something precious in order to perform a higher good. These are real sacrifices! The father would prefer to have a meal and share it with his child, but foregoes his own need. The firewoman would rather not risk her own life, but foregoes her fear and the brother would rather probably keep his own kidney and have his sister get better by other means, but again foregoes his own need for a greater good. We don't always know what good we have done by performing a sacrifice; we just have to trust that the reason is necessary…a ripple in the pond of God's Will that has further reaches than the human brain can comprehend.

In a strange way, I felt like I was making a sacrifice. I'm not saying I'm a martyr or anything like that! Let me explain. When I first realised there was something wrong, I was absolutely terrified. I was scared out of my wits at the implications and fall out should my diagnosis indeed be cancer. I did not want it at all. My courage had escaped me completely.

I prayed to God in earnest to give me back my courage and to face whatever challenge was necessary. I fell on the eternity of His mercy and surrendered to His Will, just as Mary had done when she was told she was with child. My body, mind and soul had always belonged to God. I was willing to give Him my life unconditionally if He chose to take it. His Will be done at all times. If He wanted me to continue on, then I would carry out His Will whatever it may be, even if I didn't understand it.

By the time I was diagnosed, I felt spiritually reborn. God had indeed given me courage and with it a purpose! I felt truly blessed and gave humble thanks that He had answered my prayers. With God, I could face anything! He had given me an army of angels to stand by my side and I felt closer to God than ever. So in offering my entire life to God, I felt like I had made a sacrifice: I was offering my life as a gift to whomever may need whatever I could give them without reservation or condition. I had no idea what I could give or offer, but offer myself I did; the rest was for God to arrange and dispense! Time would tell. As I said previously, God's time is not our time; *'You do not know the day or the hour'*. It is an exhortation to always be ready to 'see' the works of God because we do not always know with the eyes or ears what they are. People expect great miracles that they can visually comprehend as proof in the second they want it: walking on water, the healing of the sick, parting of the seas, rising from the dead, and so on and so forth.

Miracles don't work that way! When a person is going through a very dark time, they may pray for deliverance from their situation; but they want it immediately without input from themselves. They expect it handed to them on a plate from God. Why? Have they earned it? Do they need it or want it? God is good and God gives, but He gives what we need, not what we want, and He gives it to us at the correct time. We have to EARN it! A parent who constantly gives in to the whims of their child with nothing in return ends up with a spoilt f***ing brat who ends up filled with a sense of entitlement and no responsibility or sense of value for anything. The child just continues to expect and doesn't learn how to cope in the real world because they have never truly earned anything. And when they don't or can't get what they want, they become very extreme. angry, and blame everyone else for their own failings because they just expect that they will always have it their own way.

God gives us miracles every day and answers our prayers in many different ways. The person going through a dark time may pray for deliverance, wait a while and then give up all hopes of help from God and thus shut the door to Grace. Or the person may remain patient, maybe for many months or years, just trusting. Things may come right for that person at the appointed hour. Does that person then remember that it was God who brought it right and then give thanks? In my experience, probably not! They may not even remember that they have prayed or asked for something! So why would they remember to say thank you! Jesus expresses this perfectly in the miracle of the healing of the ten lepers. He heals all ten and sends them to the rabbi for ritual cleansing and to give praise...but only one man goes and does this. We are often very ungrateful when it comes to giving thanks when God does something for us.

I have often pondered why this should be? People expect that God will just 'appear' and just 'do stuff' for us. This is not how God primarily works. God works through human instrument and intervention (sometimes even animals), rarely by His own doing. We all are created as instruments of God's Will. God's Will may present in another person arriving in our lives just at the right time for whatever reason we may need them. Our job is to recognise that gift! It is not always easy to do as the path of the Lord is not straight and wide, as Jesus tells us! It is narrow and twisting.

Let me give you an example of this narrow, twisting road, as I believe one of my own personal experiences sums this up beautifully. I will try to keep if brief and comprehensible! I have loved animals since I was a child and always wanted to work with animals. Life took me different places; as a retail assistant, a step mother (with a dog), as a carer, as a lecturer etc. In the background I had always wanted to work with animals and preferably be a dog handler. When my hours at work dwindled, I began to volunteer at a shelter walking the dogs. Then my brother said, he wanted a puppy, as the breeder over the road to him had just bred a litter. I offered to visit the pups with my brother. I came out with my name on the list; my brother did not. A few weeks later I took Mason my new puppy home. A few months later, I was head-hunted in the park by my current boss! My path to my dream job was long and winding and took twenty-five years of the right people at

142

the right time guiding me in the right direction by God's Will. When I was offered my current job, I gave humble thanks and continue to do so every day. I love my job and it is a true gift to me.

So the path of God's works does not run in a straight and identifiable line and co-ordinate with human conceptions of linear understanding, where we like to see the immediate light at the end of the tunnel or the glowing beacon on the top of the cliff. We are all out there seeking something. But while we are seeking the light outside of ourselves, we forget to seek the light inside of us. We are all creations of God. When Genesis tells us that God made man in His own image, it speaks of the creation of the soul, not the body (Man in Hebrew generally means human kind, people-not male gender!) We are not made to physically look like God, but to spiritually look like God. So the light of God resides within us all. We all are images of the divine light and that is what allows us access to God whenever we need Him. However, not many of us know how to look in the spiritual mirror. I myself am still learning how to do this. It is a journey, not a destination.

The important thing to remember is that the divine light is in each of us, and we all are gifts to each other; gifts that God sends us all, to be lights to each other. We can illuminate someone's path when they are in the dark, or even illuminate our own path if we have the strength to do so. No one needs ever be in the dark!!! We are all beacons of hope and love to each other. Isn't that the most truly beautiful realisation?

As I looked around the Chemotherapy Day Unit on the first two days of my treatment, I saw very little despair. I saw frustration from time to time, but I mostly saw light and fight!

143

It was truly beautiful to see. I sat in a room of fighters and survivors. We were all fighting together. The more love and laughter we could bring, the stronger the fight would get. And by God's Grace and Light we would prevail. Amen.

Chapter Nine

I had obviously been advised of any of the side effects of my treatment, and this was to be expected. I had been sent home with mouthwash, cream and anti-sickness medication. This was all fine and necessary. The treatments had gone well and without issue and I hadn't felt poorly at all, but on the Wednesday, I was completely wiped out and drained! It was like a Fibromyalgia relapse type exhaustion. My monstrous appetite had dwindled somewhat, so I just ate what I fancied when I fancied it.

The most bizarre and hilarious thing I noticed the next day was my hot hair...not my scalp...just my sodding hair! From my root to about a centimetre up, my hair felt excruciatingly warm! It was bloody irritating. My scalp started to itch by the end of Wednesday night too. I was seriously thinking about 'braving the shave' already! Wearing my cap seemed to trap the heat and make it all worse. I was past caring about my hair so; it could just look like whatever...electrocuted porcupine seemed to be the reigning theme the more I lopped at my itchy napper! Whilst I felt okays and still semi-sociable, I took myself off on a tiny shopping trip while it was mid-week, quiet and less stressful (I hate shopping at the best of times!) I needed to buy some new hats and caps. My work cap was getting worn and dirty and I'd needed a new one for a while, so I took a little tootle out. Although I hadn't gone out for long, it still exhausted me more than I thought it would.

That evening, my friends Jill and Debs came around with their beautiful dog Buster. We laughed, chatted and 'played' a very old board game I'd had for years, called Dare. We didn't so much as play it as go through the quiz questions and perform the most random of dares. I seemed to get the majority of dares that involved a stop watch! We had a hilarious night! I was pleasantly tired by the end of it all and slept like a log after attempting to read some of my book in bed.

On the Thursday after a lovely long and deserved lie in, I woke to an oddly whistling nose! I had already started to lose my tiny little nose hairs! It was bloody hilarious as my nose started to belt out soft little whistling tunes randomly as I breathed. It was never the same tune either! It was only when I went and took my dogs out that I noticed how painful your nose can get without its little internal hairy jacket of warmth and protection! I could see this becoming increasingly funny but also irritating, especially as someone who worked outdoors and it was now autumn with winter approaching!

I had noticed that my nose had started to run incessantly too. It was incredibly irritating! The more it ran, the more painful my nose got and I started to get random nosebleeds. The more I wiped, the more painful my nose got. I went through tissue after tissue, which only served to heighten the discomfort and leave my nose scabby and sore. Obviously the more I wiped at it, the more it ran and the more it bled! But not wiping it was a big issue too as it would literally drip like a spontaneous tap! Gross! I swapped to pleat cotton wool to dab at my nose, interspersed with Bepanthen barrier cream to ease the sores. This was much more pleasant and gentle in dealing with the rogue nose rivers!

My mouth and throat had become dry, with the tip of my tongue becoming ridiculously sensitive: cold carbonated drinks were painful to tolerate, mint toothpaste was like sulphuric acid and anything spicy was taste bud torture! These things I can normally tolerate to a masochistic extent but not anymore! I had to swap to an extra soft toothbrush because my gums were sensitive and strawberry flavoured children's toothpaste! It didn't help that I wear a splint over my teeth for bed because I grind my teeth and this began to rub on my gums too.

Two of my other regular medications left me with a very upset stomach and reacted badly with the chemo, so, I had to stop taking them or risk being bathroom bound for hours on end and internal bleeding of the stomach. It was a bit annoying as one of the medications was an anti-flammatory painkiller for my Fibromyalgia and Hoffa's disease. This left me in more pain and a lot more limpy, but it was a small sacrifice to make in order to see the outside of my bathroom!

This all sounds very bleak, but in reality it wasn't that bad! It's more like having the tail end of a summer cold or hay fever. The biggest thing to remember is that these irritations can be managed or eased so that they don't interfere with the daily running of your life. It's not the end of the world and to be fair, there were worse symptoms to have. In reality, I felt great in myself, even if my body was adjusting to its new chemical regime. Yes, you have to make changes to things you would normally do, eat, wear or drink, even down to the usual medications you would usually take or maybe even something as simple as the time you have been accustomed to going in the shower in the past: mornings might be a chore for you now, so, you might shower later, for example. These things aren't major things to accommodate, so the more an issue that is made of them, the harder it is to cope. They are only little things and you can control them; it is within your power to do so. Feeling sorry for yourself because your nose keeps running and bleeding is entirely pointless. What does it achieve? Will despondency stop it from happening? No! Will moaning about it ease the sores? No! Will doing something proactive to ease the irritation help? Yes! By doing the things we can, we can see small improvements daily and the sores start to heal over and become less painful and the nose runs just that little bit less because it isn't over-compensating as much.

My hair, however was an entirely different matter. Losing my hair was never an issue for me from day one. I was assured that I would lose it with my type of chemotherapy. Fine. I love hats and bandanas. It wasn't an issue. My hair was short anyway, a light brown sort of colour with blonde and auburn highlights. It was usually quite soft and pliable. The chemo turned it into something akin to crispy fried seaweed in texture! It snapped off in its longer places and began to bald in other places. It was also darker and thicker. I couldn't stand the texture of it and the heat in it.

I went out for a meal on the Saturday evening with family and friends to a beautiful tandoori. I covered my hair with a scarf (I didn't want clumps of it falling out into anybody's meal!) We had an awesome night, and I was thoroughly stuffed. I couldn't wait to get the scarf off as my head was starting to overheat, even though the night was rather chilly as my mother and myself waited for the bus home.

The family attended Mass at our parish church on the Sunday and we gathered for coffee and breakfast at my mam's, as was the usual custom. My hair was getting on my nerves. It looked like a badly chewed toothbrush! After I got home and walked my dogs, I cracked a bottle of Becks Blue, dug out my barbering clippers, threw a towel around my shoulders and shaved the whole effing lot off! It felt fantastic!!! It was so liberating! The little pile of crispy fried hair on the laminate looked almost like something I'd furminated from my black Labrador, as my hair was a lot darker, almost black, than I'd first thought!

I sent a picture to a few of my family and friends. They really thought I suited it. Some comments included words such as 'gorgeous' and 'sexy'! I was definitely not ashamed of being bald. I embraced it! Most folk who didn't know about my mongrels didn't even notice as I usually wear a cap anyway. My only concern about my hair loss was not for me but for my niece who is my God-daughter. She had been concerned about me and had asked my mother what was, 'wrong' with me the previous Sunday. My mam had replied that her parents would explain and then I changed the subject and gave her a massive hug. My niece is a beautifully compassionate young lady with a wicked sense of humour. The next day, her own mother had visited me at the day unit on the first day of my treatment, as she works at the hospital where I was being treated. I asked her if she had spoken to my niece about her concerns. She had and my niece was totally unworried now. She was meeting my niece after school to take her home. This coincided with me leaving the unit after treatment, and so we met with my niece to wait for her mam. My niece was not phased as we laughed and giggled together, but I was still concerned as to how she might react to a change in my appearance. I should not have been concerned!

We all gathered at my mam's for her birthday on the Tuesday just after I had shaved my head. I was wearing a pink bandana beneath my cap, but was just wearing the bandana in my mam's warm kitchen. I had gotten there first, followed by my brother and my niece a short time later. My niece appraised the pink bandana and absorbed the fact that I looked a bit different. There was a moment of shock and worry, as if somehow the mere act of having no hair meant instant poorliness like she had probably seen on multiple cancer adverts before. As soon as I opened my mouth and cracked jokes with her, she realised that I was still the same crazy aunt and not poorly at all! We had always been close, and she was always an affectionate child, but she had seemed a lot more clingy and affectionate with me than usual as we laughed and giggled around the kitchen table.

I had always presented a strong, humorous image to my niece I think, always willing to get involved and get my hands dirty. We had worked on many of her school projects and personal craft activities together, dressed up in bunny ears, waving fairy wands just to go to the park and adventuring off to museums and libraries together. My mam taught her how to bake, just like she had done with me when I was a child (my niece could make a perfect Yorkshire pudding by the time she was four years old!) She was now approaching her teenage years and teenagers naturally begin to see the world in different ways as their horizons broaden and experience develops. I did not want her to have a single unhappy experience of me being 'poorly' during these new tender years. I was roughly the same age as she when my Aunty Barbara first fell ill, and it was difficult and painful to see her suffer so badly, even though she tried to put a brave face on it all. My teenage years were filled with grief and suffering after losing my beloved aunt to whom I was so close as a child. I did not want this for my own niece. I wanted her to be sitting in a pub with me ten years down the line laughing about my funky headgear or the fact that my hair was now curly and bright green (or whatever, if you get my point!) I certainly didn't want anyone to be upset about my situation, least of all a young girl with whom I empathised greatly, having been in a similar position myself. Yet my niece seemed to take it all in her stride knowing that I was doing well and no one was worried in any way. Her parents reassured her and dealt with it all with good humour…as I'd fully expect from my brother especially!

Having described the few shittier aspects of the treatment that I experienced, I also noticed that my skin was beautifully soft and smooth; virtually flawless! Old scars and war wounds were less prominent and noticeable. I started to gain weight…quickly (weight I had been trying to regain for years, unsuccessfully). My appetite had returned, I was generally sleeping better, I had fewer nightmares, I felt less groggy on waking up, and I had much more strength and energy! The positives far outweighed the negatives! I embraced each marvellous and miraculous positive and gave thanks to God every day, several times a day.

What was even more wonderful and positive was the love, prayers and well wishes I continuously received from all quarters…even from people I had not met! It was overwhelming in a deeply emotional and spiritual way. It gave me great pause to consider the ripples I had sent into the universe in one way or another. I had always hoped that I had acted with love and compassion as the Lord commanded. I am certainly not perfect and as prone to fits of anger and negative thoughts and actions as much as the next person, but it is our true repentance of these sins that give us the ability to correct ourselves. To paraphrase Jesus, He said that it is better to say with bad grace that you refuse to do something, but then do it with good grace anyway, rather than say with good grace that you will do something and then do not do it at all. The point is that it is perfectly natural and human to find things a chore and not want to do them and just as much natural to moan about them. But this does not mean that we can't then carry them out with a good attitude in our hearts; especially if that task is of benefit to someone. On the flip side, we should never make a promise we can't or have no intention of keeping. We might smile and say the right words that we will do something, but if we then don't do it, we are letting people down. We have put a falsehood into the universe that will only come back to bite us because it has nowhere else to go. Thoughts and words only become real when we act, either with love or hate. The church places great emphasis on good works and works of charity and for good reason…but this is not enough. The intent has to be pure and selfless, as we have spoken about previously: the rich rock-star who donates a small amount of his vast wealth compared to the single mother who donates all she can afford.

Acts of charity and good works can come in all shapes and sizes. They don't have to be extravagant, or expensive displays. Neither is it about donating your spare clothes or furniture to a charity shop; these are just excesses in your life that you don't need any more and no major sacrifice to make. Good works are essentially selfless and benefit another for no other reason than you want to help them. An example of this is the Parable of the Good Samaritan in the New Testament. He just wanted to help and was able to do so, unconditionally.

A few years ago, I was driving home from work in my van and rounded the corner just past the tiny pub on the corner of my street. As I pulled around the corner, a few people were exiting; it was only around four o'clock in the afternoon, and they had all seemed to have had a rather jolly afternoon. Seconds later, another man exited. He was absolutely intoxicated and as he hit the fresh air, he stumbled to one side and smashed his head off the rough pebble-dashed wall of the pub and fell face first like a dead tree to the concrete. I slammed my brakes on as I heard the deathly crack of his head hitting pavement and watched it bounce up again briefly before coming to rest on the cold concrete. The people with him just stood there as I abandoned my van by the side of the road, grabbed my First Aid kit and ran like a lunatic towards the injured man. A woman was dragging him by his limp arm, screaming at him to get up. I was mortified! I asked some other gentleman standing there to help me get the injured man into a sitting position so, that I could assess him. They helped me sit the man up and steady him as I introduced myself to the injured man and explained that I was a First-Aider (I actually said Canine First-Aider, but what are a few hairs between friends!) He was conscious, and I explained to him that I was going to very gently check and clean his wounds and make sure he was alright. He had a massive graze on the right side of his face and a gash over his right eye and forehead from where he had hit the concrete. I directed one of the bystanders to go into the bar for an ice pack and wet cloth, with which he duly returned. Luckily, the injured man wasn't bleeding much. I was concerned about possible concussion and other related head trauma, especially as he was so intoxicated. I cleaned him up as best I could, constantly reassuring him as he shook my hand and proffered his thanks. I advised his wife that he needed an ambulance and to be checked out properly. I was incredulous when she asked me for the number to dial! I told her to dial 999 and ask for an ambulance when she replied that 999 was only for the police! She was full of insults for her husband, and she was agitating him greatly. I kept him as calm as I could and held his hand until I heard the sounds of the sirens and bade him good health and well-being as I departed, leaving him to the professionals.

I relayed this occurrence to my friend later on, expressing my incredulity at the reluctance of his friends to help him and his own wife not even knowing the number to dial for an ambulance. My friend berated me completely for stopping my van and helping him, telling me that I should have just driven past the 'stupid drunken arsehole'. It had never occurred to me at any time to just drive past the poor man. It mattered not that he was drunk, just that he needed help! I couldn't understand my friend! If he had been injured and vulnerable, surely he would have appreciated someone, anyone stopping to help? He said he wouldn't be stupid enough to get into that state in the first place. I was horrified, arguing that it didn't matter how or why the man was injured, only that he was and therefore had needed help. My friend argued that the man could have hurt me in some way (he was incredibly protective over me and I was often mistaken for his daughter as he was considerably older than myself). I told him it was a risk, I was willing to take. He didn't understand me and I didn't understand him. We agreed to disagree! I was brought up to help when I could and I wouldn't think twice about doing so; it was purely instinctual. Most other people, I know would have done the same as I did and have done.

People often misunderstand certain conditions of the faith, especially those concerning forgiveness in the Sacrament of Reconciliation and acts of charity. They think you can merely walk into a Confessional, tell the priest that, for example, you've just killed someone and God will forgive you automatically through the Divine Intervention of the priests' absolution and that the universe can forget your sin and crime in its entirety. Sorry, but no! It doesn't work like that! You can't be forgiven for something you are not truly sorry for! This leads to the other misconception that God forgives even the most heinous of sinners, and criminals, and evil doers. God indeed does; His capacity for mercy, compassion and forgiveness is beyond human comprehension, but again, God's Grace is only available to the repentant! So even the most evil sinner can be forgiven, if they are truly sorry. In answer to a question I have been asked with reference to God's forgiveness, no, Hitler has not been forgiven and no, he is not in heaven! He never repented of his horrific crimes and, therefore cannot ever be forgiven. He certainly is not the only one!

The church teaches us that there are only two types of sin that God cannot forgive; the sin of hubris, and the sin of despondency. If we are too arrogant to accept that we need God, how can He forgive us? We need to want forgiveness, so if we don't want it or accept that we need it, how can God forgive us? If we despair of God and deliberately distance ourselves from His Grace, how then either can He forgive us? If we cannot accept Him, then He cannot forgive us. We make ourselves spiritually dead to Him. But this is where we have free will; the choice to choose God or not. The Good News is that we can choose God at any time in our lives, and He will not forsake us if we come to Him with a true and humble heart.

Many people around me had true and humble hearts. A multitude: an army of well-wishers! I couldn't even begin to express my gratitude and thanks to them all for their love and prayers; there were so many people to whom I was incredibly indebted. Many of my friends had turned back to God, or found God, or started to pray again, or learned how to pray, or began to go to church again. I had friends all over the world, of many religious or spiritual persuasions praying for me…even 'confirmed' atheists. I have pagan friends, Jewish friends, Muslim friends and atheist friends as well as Christian friends. We were all united in One Universal God, in the abundance of love that each faith preaches: to love one another. That is the universal commandment. Each person sent love in their own way…whether they believed in God or not. An atheist is not devoid of God's love, as we all carry the divine light, and God will use that light and good intention accordingly. There was so much love and light in my life. It was like walking in a perpetual glorious golden sunrise within my soul. I felt an internal beauty that I cannot even begin to describe.

It was quite an experience to witness the change in outlook from some of the people I knew. Some changes were small, some larger; or maybe I just noticed certain things more. I observed that the people I loved were laughing a lot more, they were appreciating things that they normally wouldn't comment on, such as the beauty of clouds or the soft giggle of a child; if they were irritated or perturbed, they were more ready to laugh it off or crack a joke about it rather than hang on to it and fester in it. People were letting go of their negativity more readily and moving on from bad experiences and feelings a lot more quickly than they usually did. And it wasn't that they were hiding behind false happier faces on my account either. They didn't even realise that their outlook had changed. It just seemed to be a natural transition that they were wholly unaware of. Not only was their love healing me, it was healing each other as it flowed through the universal circuit of light: God's Power Grid. Not only were people praying for me, but they were praying for each other, especially for my mam and my aunt. They were becoming more loving, compassionate and generous (which they already were!) but taking these gifts upon themselves and loving themselves that little bit more and not allowing themselves to be as easily defeated by the little things.

I had no idea whether my own outlook had influenced these little changes, I had noticed in people, but I dare speculate that maybe it had? Nothing we say or do goes out into the universe without causing an effect, as I previously reflected, so maybe I had in fact inadvertently influenced people in a positive way? These are merely my own observations and reflections so my words do not make it true or real, just an image of my own experience: nothing more, nothing less.

I had suffered for over twenty years with Fibromyalgia, anxiety and depression. It is a difficult condition to cope with and manage, and most people cannot work or have any semblance of a normal daily life. I had continued to work, to study, to develop, to exercise and to carry on as normally as I could. People must have found my illness to be quite exasperating at times when I was unable to go out for a meal because I was too exhausted or I had to come home early from a night out because I was getting anxious, paranoid and irritated. Many conversations were had about my inability to do certain things (especially when I was married). My condition was a chore for people to cope with when I was unable to function as normally as they did. People had looked at me and all they saw externally was a fit, young healthy woman, not the pain and suffering beneath my fabulous exterior! People would nod sympathetically but still be annoyed inside at me, lacking real understanding. No one ever called me brave, positive or inspirational for living with and managing my condition on a daily basis. I expected myself to cope and so did they. I accepted my limitations; they could not, because I looked 'alright'.

A few months prior to my mongrel diagnosis, my mam had been diagnosed with osteoarthritis. It is a degenerative condition and excruciatingly painful. She had been in horrendous agony, and we had kept in regular contact. I was incredibly concerned about her and how best to support her. I was the Queen of Pain Management! Her GP had not been particularly useful, so I imparted some advice that I thought she might find helpful. I telephoned her one night after she had suffered a major flare up, and she could barely walk or drive. The thought of my mam being in agony ripped my soul in two; I couldn't bear it. The sound of pain in her voice was unmistakeable when she answered the phone. You physically cannot hide true pain. She spoke of her suffering and the shock of her diagnosis (she thought she had fractured her foot). Learning that you are going to have to live with a debilitating and excruciating condition for the rest of your life is heart-breaking news for anyone. She said 'I don't know how you've coped with your Fibro all these years'. I replied simply that I had to and had chosen to. I wasn't going to be defined by my limitations or try to push past those limitations and cause a major relapse. She realised that she had to do the same. The skill was again in *'changing what you can'* to ease yourself, help yourself and be gentle and kind to yourself. The emotional and mental onslaught of physical suffering was just as crippling as the pain itself. She was surprised at how exhausted she had become and empathised with me, realising that pain is tiring as your body fights against itself and now understood why I was tired all the time.

Even though our conditions are medically very different, some of the coping strategies and treatments are similar. I supported my mam as best I could, and she learned very quickly how to operate in her new comfort zone. An essential key to this was learning to say no to things that would inevitably cause a flare up or extreme pain. My mam is a very accommodating lady and will do anything for anybody, but now she was learning to say no to things that weren't essential for her to do, whereas previously she would have done them just because she could and wanted to, such as taking my grandmother for some shopping after work and going out of her way in rush hour traffic to do so. Sitting in traffic was painful for her, so she learned to adjust to what she felt she could do, not what she thought she should do. It can be a difficult transition to make, but my mam being as stubborn and defiant as I am, made the transition very quickly. And as with me, no one called her brave, positive or inspirational for coping with what most people see as an average everyday condition.

Whether it was my stubborn and defiant crazy attitude, I don't know, all of a sudden since my mongrel diagnosis, people were calling me brave, positive and inspirational. The positive I could go with but I wasn't so sure about the brave or inspirational bit! I protested regularly at being called brave. I didn't see myself as brave. To me, bravery was something you were in the face of fear or threat. I didn't feel afraid or threatened, so how could I be brave? It bugged me excessively! Being called brave became an irrational pet-peeve and I protested without truly reflecting upon the point. So, I re-examined it more spiritually, like I do when something peeves me! I had associated bravery with BEING afraid and getting on with it regardless, so when people were calling me brave, I kept reassuring them that I was not afraid, weak or helpless or any of that sort of fiasco. It wasn't that I felt insulted or patronised at being called brave, maybe that it just wasn't the correct word to describe me.

When I looked at the Oxford Dictionary definition of 'brave' I learned very quickly that I was wrong in my assessment and association of the word. The definition is 'ready to face and endure danger or pain; showing courage'. It was not about BEING afraid, quite the contrary; it was about being wholly UNAFRAID. I suppose it's a mental state of being. In that case, I suppose I was brave! Apologies for my previous peevishness; I now accept the compliment wholeheartedly and give thanks for it. I was now beginning to see what other people were seeing in me: the stubborn defiance that got me past the school bullies, and that would not allow me to bow to peer pressure or give in to something I did not approve of or agree with. I am crazy, but principled!

All I understood was that all of a sudden I was brave, and that other people had begun to change alongside my own transformation. I don't whether it was the age-old case of people thinking 'There are people worse off than me. If she can cope with cancer then I can cope with my problems too'. I have no idea. Or whether it was just a case of love breeding love as already discussed; little mustard seeds growing out all over the world. Maybe it was a combination of both? I obviously wasn't the only person journeying through a personal transformation.

God grant us the serenity to accept the things we cannot change, to change the things that we can and the wisdom to know the difference.

Chapter Ten

I was at work when my Breast Nurse Pauline telephoned me. I was driving, so transferred her to hands-free. She explained that she had forgotten to tell me that I needed to see the oncologist after my first round of chemo, so, I needed to attend the hospital that Friday, just before my next round of treatment on the Monday. Part way through the conversation, my sat-nav blared out loudly, drowning out Pauline's voice. I was locating a new dog on my route and my sat-nav was taking me miles away. Pauline burst out laughing as my sat-nav sent me loud commands. I was going to the hospital on the Friday anyway to have my bloods taken, so popping in to see my oncologist was not a problem. Pauline had assured me that the appointment was purely routine between her bursts of laughter at my frustrated sat-nav!

I had undergone an MRI on my spine, lumbar and liver on the day of my blood transfusion, just before my first round of chemo. I hadn't heard anything about results so there was that awareness of it all as I prepared to see my oncologist. I had gone with the theory that no news is good news. I hadn't felt like anything was wrong in those areas, but there is always that concerned consciousness that creeps in. As long as we don't allow ourselves to be consumed with worry and learn to accept whatever challenges come our way with strength and courage, we can cope and live just as easily as always. I prayed to God to maintain my strength and courage.

My appointment was for 10.30am on the Friday. When I arrived, the tiny waiting room was very busy with only a few spare seats. I knew the clinic wouldn't be running to schedule; it never does. Not that this was particularly an issue in itself. Issue was my claustrophobia and anxiety! The waiting room started to get incredibly busy and I began to feel suffocated the longer I sat there. I ended up getting squashed into a corner. An elderly couple sat to the left of me, quite in my personal space. They did nothing but fidget with newspapers, bags and coats for the entire time they were sat there. People who fidget make me anxious and irritated. A man opposite me sat there with a gormless open-mouthed grin on his face; his jaw had dropped so wide I thought, he was posing to catch flies like a Venus Fly trap. It's so impolite! I thought my head was going to pop by the time I got called in fifty minutes later!

The nurse gave me a front opening gown and asked me to get changed. I knew the drill! I duly undressed to the waist down, donned the gown and waited for my doctor. He arrived few moments later and asked to examine me. I assumed the position lying on the bed with my arms above my head. He began to examine the offending breast, feeling around gently. He asked if I had noticed any change. I said jubilantly that I had and that the tumour was definitely smaller. He agreed and said, 'It's working!' He then asked me to get dressed, and he would come and have a chat with me.

After a few moments he returned and asked me about side effects of my treatment. I explained that they had been minimal and mostly unobtrusive. I told him I felt great, and he was very happy with this. He then told me that they were adding a new therapy to my treatment which I would receive every other cycle. It was a drug therapy called Denosumab to help with the spread to my bones and to protect my bones from the effects of chemotherapy, especially as I was post-menopausal. After our brief but jubilant conversation, I tootled off to phlebotomy to have my bloods taken, where again I was surrounded by moaners and fidgeters. The elderly gentleman to the right of me did nothing but moan that he was five people behind me and that he would be 'here all day!' and 'why did he need another blood test anyway?' His wife was very patient with him despite her obvious frustration with his complaining. Her voice sounded drained as she explained things to him. I was grateful to be called into the little room for my bloods taken because he was getting on my nerves!

After the hospital, I went and did my shopping and promised myself a leisurely afternoon. As leisurely as it was, my phone never stopped beeping or ringing as I imparted the good news to my family and friends. It was truly lovely to be able to impart positive news. A lot of people were praying for me and sending love so, it was magnificent to be able to share the fruits of their labour. People had their own lives and issues to worry about; it was incredibly kind and generous of them to worry about me, so anything I could do to minimise their concerns was a blessing.

The rest of the weekend passed without incident. I remained well and active, spending time with my step-daughter, doing a spot of shopping, attending Mass and spending time with my family. I was due my second round of chemo on the Monday, so plenty of rest was needed and gotten. On the Sunday night, I prepared my chemo bag, which was basically a bag of puzzle books and snacks! Even though the hospital brought lunch around, I was so hungry that I needed the extra munchies! I packed enough snacks to feed an army (or just for me for breakfast!) which of course I packed enough for my mam too. I can't say I slept well that night, however. The steroids gave me insomnia and horrific cramp down my right arm again. It was indeed a very restless night, so I was exhausted the next morning when my mam picked me up at nine in the morning to go to the hospital.

My nurse came into the waiting room and escorted me and my mam to the treatment room. She had just come back from a lovely holiday abroad and looked tanned and rejuvenated. Once in the treatment room she asked me about side effects and explained the new therapy I was going to receive as I had asked her about it. As usual, she was pleased that I was fully conversant and participant in my treatment, ready to ask questions and understand what was going on. I knew that it would be a long day again as the treatments are administered in staggered doses over several hours. I was receiving four different therapies that day. The first was the new therapy which was to be administered by injection. The nurse asked if I would prefer it in my arm or tummy. I said arm because I'm ticklish just as my mam laughed 'Good Lord not her tummy and not anywhere near her belly button, or she'll throw up!' The nurse burst out laughing at my weirdness.

Yes, that's right, I have a phobia of belly buttons! I didn't actually realise this until I was about sixteen years old. My then boyfriend bear hugged me from behind and accidentally stuck his finger in my belly button as he did. I projectile vomited all over his best friend who was standing in front of me and felt creeped out for days! I can't bear my belly button to be touched!!! My darling niece used to like torturing me when she was little by poking her own belly button as she chased me around the dining room table shouting 'Aunty Rach, I'm going to get you!' It's hard to run while you're retching!

So into the arm went my new therapy. I'm not bothered by injections but this one was quite large and smarted a little as it went in, but probably because it was a bigger dose of drugs than your average flu jab! The cannula was then inserted into the back of my right hand in order to receive my next three therapies. Once the cannula was in, my mam tootled off to the kitchen to make coffee and retrieve biscuits while we waited for the first of my therapies to arrive from the pharmacy. Then we started on the puzzles as the room slowly started filling up with other guests. The nurse intermittently kept proffering answers as she buzzed around the room doing her job.

A lovely gentleman called Gary took a seat to the left of me. He reminded me of a former student I'd had, whom I held in high regard. He was balding (not chemo induced) with a beard and around the same age as me. Through indiscreet conversations with the nurse, we discovered he was ex-army and extremely intelligent with an excellent sense of humour and compassion. He had been sat for a while waiting for his therapy to arrive, and he was visibly bored. His hands and legs were restless and his eyes were searching. He had no one with him to converse with or comfort him or relieve his boredom. As my mother and I pondered our puzzles and laughed with each other, he caught my gaze and announced 'It's bloody boring, isn't it?' with a bit of a heavy sigh. We agreed that sitting on your own for hours on end staring at the same four walls was indeed boring! I had a spare puzzle book and pencil in my 'chemo bag,' so I offered it to him in order to keep his mind occupied and simultaneously distracted. He accepted gratefully and threw himself into the Code breakers, sometimes chatting to us as he puzzled his way through the codes, and sometimes just puzzling in silence. He was very kind to me and offered me a drink of his Lucozade when I got a bit too warm. It's the smallest gestures that really count.

The time seemed to fly quite quickly despite treatment being an all-day job. It's literally an eight-hour stint at the hospital. Obviously not everyone is there that long; some maybe for minutes as they have a single injection, some for maybe an hour or two and like me, some are there for a full day out! My therapies had ended by around four o'clock and as I got up to leave, Gary handed me back the puzzle book. I asked him to keep it as he still had another hour of his treatment to go. We exchanged goodbyes, and we both said that we hoped we would see each other again, chemo schedules permitting.

Again, I had rarely seen a miserable person in the treatment room. We all seemed quite buoyant and the fantastic nurses helped to maintain this humour we had amongst us all. My mam and I had seen more relatives crumble than the afflicted people. Yes, we all had our little niggles about our treatment and the way it affected us, but from what I had seen, people tended to cope well with these. One quite prevalent thing I saw on that particular day was a lot of people sitting with their hands in hot water prior to treatment. I had been offered hot water too, but I did not need it. My veins are usually very co-operative, and usually give blood easily or accept cannulas easily. Some people don't have that luxury and their veins need a bit of warm water coaxing to come forth. I felt bad for these people; it's difficult enough without the added aggravation of non-co-operative veins and having to sit with your hands in water for half an hour or so…unable to have a brew!

It was only my second cycle, so I think I was the newest to the day unit at that point. Others had been receiving therapy for longer. For example, Gary was receiving his fifth therapy when we met. He explained how the first two had been alright for him, but by the third and fourth he had really felt the exhaustion kicking in. It was to be expected really, despite any best efforts to combat it with rest and sleep. The insomnia of the steroids certainly wasn't a help when it came to being stupidly tired!

I felt fine when I got home so was determined to go to work the next day, despite plans being in place for me not to be in the event, I felt too crap. I did not feel crap, so off to work I would go! I was tired and groggy after a sleepless steroid night of muscle cramps in my arm, but I didn't feel poorly or anything like that. I really enjoyed my day at work, but by goodness was I floored when I got home! I was so tired I started to go blind and could barely keep my eyes open. I was staggering all over the house, unable to function correctly. Some of my work takes place in the evenings, so once that was done, I gave up the fight against my eyelids and went to bed where I slept like a log despite the lingering cramp in my right arm.

I slept quite alright the next night too. Having Fibromyalgia, you rarely get a pain free night where you don't have to get up and stretch or move before you seize up, but this is quite normal for me. Usually, I wouldn't be able to get back to sleep, but I did without issue. The next night was not the same story! I was in agony with my diseased knee and my back pain was crippling. I could barely lie down let alone get comfortable in any way. My beloved dogs have a tendency to want to help when I'm in pain, so climbed on the bed to comfort me. As loving as they are, it didn't help! They tried to cuddle in close, or lie on top of me (they aren't small boys either!) At one point I was almost snuggled onto the floor, when Mason cuddled hard into my back! I was up and down all night in agony. I finally relented at seven in the morning, and crawled out of bed like a drugged and beaten Neanderthal. The dogs were over the moon as they got their breakfast a bit earlier!

I managed to get my shopping done, return home, and basically rest all day. The pain in my knee wouldn't ease up at all. I tried a hot bath, painkillers, elevation and all the usual remedies, but that's the joy of Hoffa's Disease: it's horrifically painful and completely incurable. Not that the pain stopped me from eating at all! There seemed to be no limits to my insatiable hunger! I ate just about every two hours or I'd get grumpy and distracted!

In the meantime, people were telling me how great and well I looked. I must have looked like a right bag of shite for ages! It was strange to be so complimented frequently; I was completely humbled by it all but accepted it graciously. It was nice to feel like I was progressing in the eyes of others and not just myself. I know I had looked frail and unwell, and this had been long commented upon, but now, I was being told differently and it matched how I felt about myself for a change. I had stopped running from myself. I had stopped hiding my light under a bushel.

Side effects were still minimal, and for that I was grateful. A few days after the second cycle, the soft stubble that was the rest of my hair started to moult. It constantly looked like I had just come out of the barber's with tiny fried jet-black hairs shedding all over me. I seemed to be constantly itchy around my neck and shoulders as these tiny little demons wound their way inside my clothes to irritate me! Every time I took my cap off, there was a poufy cloud of fine fried hair around my face. I had done a pretty crap job of shaving it originally in the first place, so there were some longer uneven bits at the back that just looked a mess and aggravated my OCD. So the clippers came out again!

The first week saw the return of horrific heartburn. The first few days were particularly harsh, but taking antacids after meals and before bed really helped, as did milk and cream cheese funnily enough! Coffee was a big aggravator, as was anything even remotely spicy or peppery (my favourite things!) I could put up with this though, as long as there was an antidote! And it was only for a few days anyway as the heartburn tended to tail off after four or five days. The first week also saw the return of a couple of tiny mouth ulcers and the super-sensitive taste buds…until the splint I wear to stop grinding my teeth caused a painful lesion underneath my tongue. It was far from pleasant and I had to stop wearing my splint for bed. Regular use of a salt rinse and medicated mouthwash sorted this out perfectly after a few days, and all was well again!

The second week saw the return of the random nosebleeds. Some were heavier than others, and occurred at the most inconvenient of times…not that a nosebleed is ever convenient to be fair! But going up the stairs to bed because you are ready for sleep and then your nose exploding is really not convenient; I mean, you can't exactly then go to sleep with your nose pissing of blood! Or when I was getting ready to take my dogs out for a walk, bending over to tie my shoes and then my nose starting to bleed is really not convenient either...not for me or my dogs!

Again these were minor irritations: there are more horrific things to suffer with than a bit of heartburn or a few nosebleeds here and there. I considered myself to be very blessed. I was achy and sore, but this was nothing new to me as a Fibromyalgia sufferer, especially with the approach to winter and colder, damper weather. I can imagine that for a person who is used to being in the full bloom of health on a daily basis, these things would be more than just a minor irritation; rather a major blight on their wellness and well-being both physically and psychologically.

I was not without assaults on my psychology either. I am as human as the next person and vulnerable to the same doubts, fears and insecurities. By the end of the first week, my emotions were a bit raw. I had kept naturally upbeat, but for one reason or another I became depressed. Losing my hair had never bothered me in the slightest, but a creeping doubt had set in about something I struggled to put my finger on for a few days. My hair was hitting that sparse, soft stubbly stage where shiny patches of scalp shone through. I looked in the mirror and for the first time, I saw 'a cancer patient': I saw my Aunt Barbara and everything that had terrified me back then. I was living my worst fear; a fear that had developed twenty-five years before. Yet, I was not afraid or worried in my soul; it was all in my head; remembered agonies. I was being tempted into doubting God.

Now, a lot of people believe in the existence of a 'good force' even if they do not believe in God, but in discussions with people, some of them do not believe in the existence of an 'evil force' and certainly not in the devil. Some people who believe in God also do not believe in the devil. The universe is made up of physical laws of opposites e.g., the opposites of magnets, electricity, protons and neutrons, etc. The universe could not function without the balance of opposites. If God exists, then, so must the devil. If good exists, then, so must evil. If God manifests through the actions of mankind, then so does the devil. And if God manifests to a person in a private spiritual communication, then so does the devil.

I pondered my feelings as I prepared to attend Mass. I could not understand why I felt as downbeat as I did and worried about something that had certainly not been an issue for me previously. I berated myself for being so out of sorts and filled with doubt. And then it hit me. I was being tempted by the Evil One. He wanted me to doubt, to fail, to throw God aside and to be miserable. I was horrified! He was whispering feelings of doubt and fear in my ear, reminding me of past horrors and giving me excuses to be afraid; tempting me to give in and give up. How did you know it was him I hear you say? The answer is as simple as I can give it: he has the ability to suck the joy right out of your soul, even when you are at your happiest and most joyful. He hates that and will do everything to destroy your joy. When God speaks it is to enhance your joy and give you hope and your soul feels peaceful and untroubled. That's the difference. When you are full of joy and peace, God enhances it and you begin to share Mustard Seeds. When you are full of joy and peace, the devil will tempt you into misery, which leads to sin and doubt…and self-loathing.

I had been well accustomed to hearing God, but I had not been accustomed to hearing or recognising the subtle little whispers of the devil. The joy at realising it was indeed he was almost enough to send him back to hell in itself; the devil hates it when we see him for whom he really is and confront him with the depth of our faith. I called upon the Lord and St Michael the Archangel and recited The Lord's Prayer until my soul was purged of the evil that the devil had tried to plant. I would not doubt. I would not fail. I would not be afraid. The devil was banished. I attended Mass with a warriors' heart and gave thanks for my salvation. And when I attended Mass, the prayer of St Michael the Archangel was printed on the Mass sheet. I was jubilant and thankful. It was almost as though God and I were of one mind. The devil would not overwhelm me.

Chapter Eleven

I went to the hospital for my bloods taken prior to my third round of chemo, as was the drill. When I arrived however, they'd forgotten to book me in. The phlebotomist tried to ring through to the chemotherapy day unit but couldn't get an answer. She was really apologetic, but I assured her that it wasn't a problem, and that my bloods could be done on the day of my chemo and all it meant was a small delay to my treatment, which again wasn't exactly a major fiasco.

When I arrived on the Monday for my chemo, it did in fact seem to be a fiasco from the minute we all got there! As usual, I was cannulised and had my bloods taken. Then ensued a long-drawn-out period of waiting of several hours. Nobody was getting any of their treatments…at least no one expecting chemotherapy.

I'd been doing puzzles and having munchies with my mam for a couple of hours, and then she tootled off to the kitchen to make us a brew, when I heard one of the patients complaining to the nurse that she had been there for ages and not had her treatment and never usually had to wait as long, etc. The nurse explained that the chemotherapy machine was being serviced and that because of this, none of the treatments could be prepared until they were finished. Patients started ringing families to change plans, collection times, etc. I explained all I'd heard to my mam when she came back with our coffees. Even I was getting frustrated by this point! My first treatment of Perjeta arrived at 12.45 pm, about three hours later than usual, just as lunch arrived.

When a treatment is late, it has a knock-on effect on other treatments a patient may be having, as the line has to be flushed with a saline drip between treatments, which obviously adds time onto the day which is already long and tiring. I was almost at the end of my second treatment which was Herceptin, when the nurse came to take more bloods from me as the first lot from the morning had haemolysed (clotted) by the time they'd caught up with themselves from the morning fiasco. About half an hour later the nurse came back to set up my line flush and tell me that my bloods showed higher than desirable liver function. My liver function had been slightly higher since starting chemo, and this round of bloods was a bit higher still, so, she needed to check with my oncologist that it was safe to administer my chemo…except she couldn't reach him.

By this point I was demented! I was pacing the floor with my IV stand in my right hand. I had cramp in my feet and my back was aching. There was only myself and another lady receiving treatment by this time in the afternoon, as hers had also been delayed. She was as equally demented as I was, but we were both congenial about it. After all, it was not the fault of the nurses, and they did their level best and beyond to sort everyone out expediently. An hour or so later, the nurse came back with my chemo, having spoken to my oncologist who was quite happy for me to have the treatment. It turned out to be a bloody long day, not getting home until about 6.30 pm, and I was absolutely exhausted, but otherwise perfectly fit and well. Before I left the hospital, I made sure that I was booked in for my next lot of bloods for round four!

By the end of the night, I started to get random sensations in my hands and feet; tingling, patchy numbness and burning…like hot frostbite! But it also felt like I was wearing woolly gloves, so my hands became virtually uncontrollable in their clumsiness. A common phrase to be heard from my lips when I was handling anything was 'For fucks sake!' My left hand is damaged and clumsy already but the chemo made it ridiculous! I went to stroke the cat and instead ended up twatting her in the face with the back of my hand. She wasn't impressed. Unscrewing lids is now like a game of spinning tops because I generally send them spinning across the floor. My hands drive me mental!

I had been having severe insomnia over the days I was taking the steroid pre-meds, so opted to take decaffeinated coffee to the hospital for my chemo day out for round four. I took a jar to leave in the kitchen should either staff or patients need it. Round four passed blessedly without incident and very quickly, except that my hands were cold and my veins weren't playing so the nurse cannulised the side of my wrist, leaving my thumb in agony for days afterwards! I asked how my bloods were, and they were good (that's as much input as I got!) My mam, and I did our usual puzzles, and chatted on and the treatments were administered pretty much one directly after another without any significant delay. I was out of the hospital by about 3.30 pm and shopping with my mam by 4.00 pm! I slept really well and without the usual arm cramps, although the chemo did make me tired and a bit groggy as is normal for a couple of days after. I had the usual heartburn and weird tingly sensitive tongue thing and horrific amounts of pain in my joints and muscles as I'd also had the Denosumab injection. It was like having the bends! Yet on I battled!

I went to work as usual, went Christmas shopping, wrapped up presents, bought myself a new Christmas tree, went out for meals, prepared the Christmas games and quizzes, went to Mass each Sunday and looked forward to my friend's wedding and to Christmas with my family. For me, it was business as usual. The thing I looked forward to most was attending Mass and breakfasting with my family afterwards every Sunday. I had been unable to go to Mass for months because I was so poorly before, but now I feel fantastic. I still struggle physically with things because my muscles and joints have never really co-operated with me, but I won't let it hold me down or stop me from trying. Some people don't even try in the first place because they don't want to fail, but by not even trying, the only person you fail is yourself because life is full of lessons, and we are not expected to achieve perfection first time, every time. God is a patient teacher and parent.

I had seen my oncologist just after round four of my chemo, and he wanted to do the examination of the boob thing, so, I donned the 'gown of exposure' and assumed the position as he gently felt around the offending boob. There had been more shrinkage so, he was very happy. At this point I asked him a question. I asked him if it was significant that the pain I had previously had in my ribs and sternum was now virtually non-existent. He smiled broadly at me and said, 'Yes'. I said, 'So that's a good sign then?' He replied, still smiling 'It's a very good sign!' He said I needed a CT scan, and that he would see me again in a few weeks.

I had the scan a few days later on the Tuesday about a week before my fifth round of chemo. I went to the hospital on the Friday for my usual bloods, but yet again they'd forgotten to book me in! The nurses get stupidly busy on the ward and so the phlebotomist had trouble reaching them. I reassured her that I would just get them done on the day of my chemo and it was no big deal. So, I went Christmas shopping instead!

My mother and I duly arrived at the hospital on the Monday morning for round five of my chemo. I was cannulised and had my bloods taken very swiftly, having warmed my hands up on a mini hot water bottle prior to vein examination! The cannula was inserted comfortably into the back of my right hand, and so, I waited for the first of my treatments. There again seemed to be some delay to the treatments being administered. The morning patients who were expecting only single injections or a single dose of tablets were sitting waiting for several hours, like myself, other than their usual minutes. Patients started to moan and complain, questioning the staff. As far as I was concerned, it would take as long as it took! Things invariably happen that might delay things and it was no major deal and certainly not the fault of the staff who were as equally frustrated! There were patients still in the waiting room way past their appointment time because the nurses had nowhere to seat them in the treatment rooms.

It turns out that the comedy of errors contained three delaying fiascos, the first one being that one of the oncologists had forgotten to sign the prescriptions for the chemotherapy patients due that day. So the oncologist had to be tracked down, the scripts sent to be authorised, the scripts sent back and then logged onto the Chemotherapy Care System. Problem number two; the Chemotherapy Care System had crashed so no one needing chemo was getting it because the team that mixed the chemotherapy didn't know who was getting what! Obviously this delayed the mixing and sending to the pharmacy to be dispensed. Problem number three; the maintenance team were refurbishing the pharmacy, so the pharmacy couldn't receive any deliveries in order to dispense them to the departments requiring them.

On this occasion my mother and I omitted to do our usual puzzles. It seemed that neither of us had our usual mental energy. It wasn't exactly an issue because me and my mam get on like a house on fire and can always find something to chat about, whether it be holiday memories, family issues or my research. My mam is fascinated by my religious research into early Christianity and the discoveries I have made. And so, we chatted as the nurses flitted around us with frustration and desperation. It was again another long day.

My treatments had all been completed by 5 pm and all I was waiting for was the removal of my cannula. The nurses were still extremely busy treating patients who had been significantly delayed. So, me and my mam sat, waited, and chatted. Then about half an hour later one of the nurses came into the treatment room to see to another patient and looked over at my IV stand. 'Oh, you're finished,' she said. 'I'll just put your flush through'. I told her that I'd finished my last flush. 'Oh, my goodness! All you need is your cannula out then!' she exclaimed. 'I'm really sorry! I hadn't realised. I totally forgot!' She was filled with panic and stress and I had seen her on the verge of tears several times during the day. At one point I had asked her if she was ok, and she said she was 'pissed off'. Understandable! She was still very apologetic as she gently removed my cannula. 'Don't worry about it,' I said, 'There are people in here who need you too. I'm not the only patient in your care. You do a fantastic job, and you've been crazy all day playing catch up. What's a little wait to me?' She looked at me with a humbled look on her face and said, 'You're so lovely. Some patients really aren't like you and complain about everything'. I felt very humbled at that point. I wasn't there to make their lives difficult. They were there to help me and the least I could do was to support their role.

It made me reflect once again on the virtue of patience. I discussed earlier on how people want God to 'act' for them there and then and how when they didn't get what they wanted immediately they lost faith and hope and became spiteful and jaded. They blame God. We can't always have what we want in the here and now…and what we want isn't always good for us. Some things we want might just be a passing flight of fancy that we then care nothing about after the fact of getting it. Christmas is a prime example of this!

When I was a child, as Christmas approached, my brother, and I would get catalogues from Argos and start going through them, picking toys and circling them, discussing them and generally getting very excited about it all. My parents would observe this ritual with fascination. Obviously we never got every single thing we circled or discussed because that would have been madness and teach us nothing. What our parents did was to observe which toys we alighted upon and discussed the most and were least likely to change our minds over a week before Christmas. This is sensible parenting! So, everything we got for Christmas was a toy we would use and play with regularly and not just sit there collecting dust.

My cousin is a prime example of a child who pined on for weeks before Christmas one year for a certain gaming computer, wanting the newest and most expensive experience possible. My aunt duly went and acquired this gift for him. Two weeks before Christmas he declared that he no longer wanted it and wanted another more expensive model instead. Well, my aunt had already bought it! She told him to swivel, and there were tantrums. From what I recall she had to exchange it after Christmas because he made such a fuss.

If God gave us what we wanted each time every time, where would our sense of gratitude be? Where would our sense of worth be? We get because we've earned it. People who get without earning it are selfish and ungrateful people who just expect the universe to drop all good things into their laps and tantrum when it doesn't. I think these people are beyond pathetic with no sense of responsibility. They wander through life feeling completely blameless for bad things that happen to them and ultimately blame God when there is no one left to blame. The buck ultimately stops with us as humans because we are instruments of God's will on earth. We are responsible for each other and ourselves. And people still ask, 'Where was God when I needed Him?' Standing right in front of you, you pillock!

So, we must have patience as God will make things right for us in His own time, when we actually need it to and not just because we want it to on a brief flight of fancy. My own journey is necessarily one of patience. My diagnosis is that it is, 'incurable but treatable'. I know that I am not going to heal sufficiently overnight. It is a lesson in also being patient with myself and not expect more than I am capable of physically or mentally. I had to learn to be gentler with myself.

A few days after my fifth round of chemo, I had a consultation with my oncologist for my CT scan results. I'd felt pretty upbeat prior to the consult but then my anxiety started to spiral. This is quite normal and I expected to feel tense. My mam had wanted to come with me but I assured her that I was fine to go on my own and I'd keep her posted. I felt very positive about it and so did she. My doctor didn't need to examine me on this occasion, just chat about my scan. He told me that the lesions present around my ribs and sternum were under control, my bloods were phenomenal and obviously there was shrinkage in the boob area which could be seen and felt without the use of a scan. He strongly recommended a mastectomy and then further targeted therapy treatment on a three-week cycle. He asked me if this was ok, grinning broadly. I was over the moon!

I practically skipped out of the hospital praising Jesus! I got in my car and immediately rang my mam. She was at work, but her boss and colleagues had been a mountain of support to both her and I, and they were all waiting anxiously for news. My mam answered the phone with a shaking voice asking what was wrong because I usually just sent a text after I'd seen my doctor. I told her nothing was wrong, and it was all good news and explained that everything was under control, etc. She was shaking with anxiety and then relief and I could hear her trying to control her sobs. She was praising Jesus in the corridor! It was a major relief because controlling the bone mongrels was, I had been advised, the complicated bit. I wasn't bothered about having a mastectomy. If it needed to be done then so be it. It was God's will. I told her to straighten her make up before going back into the office to impart the good news, or people would think something was wrong! She was going out that evening for a Christmas meal, and it was lovely to be able to give her good news to celebrate with her friends.

Good news was an excellent Christmas gift, and I was looking forward to spending time with my family. My aunt, uncle, cousin, and granny were coming to my mam's for Christmas lunch. I was (and always am) the quiz master, so I had plenty of entertainment to offer our guests. We went to Mass on Christmas Eve and then went to the local pub for a family drink afterwards. It was my first alcoholic drink in months. I had a pint of lager and the first mouthful was disgusting! I was surprised at how much I disliked the taste considering I loved my beer previously. I didn't overdo it though. I went to my mam's for our usual whiskey and green ginger drinks, which we always do on Christmas Eve. We have a drink for my Aunt Barbara, and her favourite was whiskey, and green ginger. This year was the twenty-fifth anniversary of her passing, so we drank to her. I then took myself home and relaxed with my dogs and cats in front of a movie and eventually fell asleep on the couch because I was in too much pain to get up the stairs to bed. I woke up on Christmas Day feeling slightly like I'd been hit by a bus, but that wasn't going to stop me from enjoying myself and eating a great deal of delicious food!

I loaded the car with my dogs and presents. My dogs always visit my mam on Christmas Day for their presents and munchies, as they always get the meat trimmings. Usually, I would walk to my mam's with them and start drinking early, but given my knee injury, I drove there with my dogs and me and my mam had a lovely morning opening presents before I took my dogs home and came back. We had an absolutely lovely day chilling out and playing games. My mam's dinner was phenomenal as always. My mam's partner loved playing my version of Rapidough, and he eventually won. You can play with Play-doh and plasticine at any age! It's all about the fun.

On Boxing Day, I chilled out with the dogs and watched movies and mostly ate chocolate! I was off work, so I was at liberty to rest as I needed. On the Friday I had a busy day. My kitten Eli was going to the vets for an operation to have two teeth removed4On the Friday I had a busy day. My kitten Eli was going to the vets for an operation to have two teeth removed. His canines on the left-hand side had grown in wrong and were impinging his ability to eat. Once I had dropped him at the vets, I had to go to the hospital for my bloods as I was due my final round of chemo on New Year's Eve. So duly I dropped a very stroppy cat off at the vets and tootled off to get my bloods done.

A few hours later, I received a phone call from one of the nurses on the chemo unit. She asked me if I was alright in a very concerned voice as I'd just had bloods done that morning. I assured her I was fine and asked why. She explained that my white blood count was too low and my neutrophil levels were half of what they should be. Obviously they check on the patient if bloods come back with concerns! I checked my temperature for her and it was in the normal range and I reassured her once again that I was fine. She reassured me that it was just from the chemo that my levels were low, but was surprised because previously they had been fine. Throughout my chemo I had been taking Manuka honey capsules but had run out prior to round five. I wondered if that could have also accounted for a drop in my immune system. My mam went into a bit of a panic, when I told her that my neutrophils were low but I assured her I was fine. We were going to her partner's new house the next night for Chinese food, and she was concerned because he had been poorly with a bad cold and thought I shouldn't go, but I was fine. Yes, my immune system was limited but it still existed, and he wasn't exactly ill. So, I thoroughly enjoyed my meal and the company as I normally would!

Monday rolled around and me and my mam rocked up to the hospital for my sixth and final round of chemo. They took my bloods again to check my neutrophils, and I waited for my first treatment, which was the Denosumab injection. This was done pretty swiftly and then it was over an hour later that I was hooked up to the Perjeta. It was a late start at 12.20 pm, three hours after I had arrived but this was no big deal; we did our puzzles and ate munchies! Although I had started late, the therapies progressed swiftly, and I was done by 4 pm. Then I was allowed to compile my success board on the unit!

Each patient who finishes chemo is allowed to compile their success board. There is a little cupboard on the unit where one can stick things and write a message and have their photograph taken. I wrote my message, 'Yippee kai ay mother fuckers!' and had photos with my mam and some nurses. Although my treatment was not over by a long shot, it was a milestone!

My mam got very emotional. We saw one of the breast nurses who had examined me at the very beginning of my journey, and she was over the moon to see me. She told me that my doctor was really pleased with my progress and had told her how well I was doing. She was pleased that surgery was now possible. It was what my mam needed to hear. It's all well and good for me to hear it, but my mam also needed that positive input. My mam just gushed about how proud she was of me. A lot of people were very proud of me and called me an inspiration. I felt very humbled. They were amazed that I was carrying on as normal, battling through the symptoms and side effects, and generally being no different to how I usually am. My mam said I made having cancer look easy.

Having cancer isn't easy, but neither is living with any sort of illness: there are people on dialysis; people who have to inject themselves with insulin; people who have to apply various creams and lotions, or take medications to cope with and monitor a condition. The condition just becomes a part of your lifestyle and has to be accommodated. Yes, you have to adjust your life, but as I have personally discovered, my changes were for the better and helping me to heal. I am making more allowances for myself when I need to and treating myself better. I don't think about the things I can't do; I think about the things that I can do. I live life. I don't sit around moping about 'what ifs'. And I've long passed giving a flying f*** what anyone else thinks. I am me. This is who I am.

I see the wonder of God everywhere. I see the love He has for us and I don't ever feel alone or defeated. I thank Him frequently for every blessing. Everything is possible with God. I offered Him the entirety of my being to do His will and I trust in Him in ways that words cannot express. I bear witness to the work that He does through others, as I have been sent many angels on my journey to watch over me. I have seen a massive outpouring of love, not just for me but for those around me. That is the kind of love that God intended for us to share amongst each other; unconditional compassion, for always and not just in times of need. If my own personal lesson helps to teach others the value, and necessity of unconditional love, then I thank God for finding me worthy to share His message. In Divine Love there is Divine Healing.

So, let us reflect. I accepted the things I cannot change: the need for the treatment such as chemotherapy, targeted therapies and surgery. I accepted that I would have side effects. I changed the things that I could: my diet, my medication, my lifestyle and my attitude. The wisdom to know the difference? Working in partnership with God. Listen to Him. If you keep fighting the same things, and are not winning, it is obviously something you cannot change. So change what you can. Acceptance isn't about giving up; it's about letting go of unnecessary baggage. God will always lighten your load if you are prepared to put it down. We all hold on to baggage we don't need. I wasn't going to carry baggage of misery around because of my diagnosis. I didn't want or need to be miserable and neither did I want that for anyone else around me. While love exists, so does healing.

God grant me the serenity to accept the things I cannot change, to change the things that I can and the wisdom to know the difference.

Amen

Printed in the USA
CPSIA information can be obtained
at www.ICGtesting.com
LVHW020406170923
758334LV00009B/206